INTERIOR DESIGN
with Ken Edwards

GILL AND MACMILLAN
and
RADIO TELEFÍS ÉIREANN

Published by
Gill and Macmillan Ltd
Goldenbridge
Dublin 8
and
Radio Telefís Éireann
Donnybrook
Dublin 4
© Ken Edwards 1990
0 7171 1815 0
Edited by Roberta Reeners
Designed by Design Image, Dublin
Colour photographs courtesy of Arco Kitchens
Colour origination by Kulor Centre Ltd
Printed by Criterion Press, Dublin

CONTENTS

INTRODUCTION

Designing interiors for your own home can be both enjoyable and rewarding. It is wonderful to see your scheme take shape before your eyes and become something that once was only in your imagination. It can also be most frustrating. I'm sure you have been to the local wallpaper shop, only to be totally mesmerised and hypnotised by the vast numbers of patterns and colours available. The more samples you see, the more difficult it is to make a choice. This happens to everyone and it is only natural that you should find it difficult to make up your mind.

The real trick is to know what you are looking for. This immediately reduces the choice available and makes it much easier. But how do you know what you are looking for?

Have you seen what you think you want in a glossy magazine? Are you going for a fashion colour of the moment? Have you pulled an idea out of the air? There are many ways to success, but a little knowledge is usually a great help.

Every room in your house can tell a story. It will give you ideas if only you know how to listen to it. Allow each room to get you on the right track. Learn to recognise what it is saying and how you can make use of it. If you do, you can overcome many of the room's shortcomings, ending up with something practical and pleasant.

This book gives you ideas rather than colour schemes. Colour is a very personal thing and if you like red and green together, who am I to say it is wrong? The colours you choose should express your personality and tastes. The interior design ideas here are meant to guide you along the right track.

Take your courage in both hands and have a go. Don't be put off by the difficulties or even fear. I know that making a mistake can be very expensive, but don't allow the problem to outweigh the enjoyment you can get in creating a background to your type of living.

Most of the interior design books or magazines give beautiful examples and ideas mainly for baronial mansions, converted millhouses or places with great character. Most of us, however, live in ordinary, simple houses. It is difficult to relate our houses to the pictures in the glossy magazines, even if they are fascinating and beautiful. This book is about *your* house - the simple 'three up - two down' effort with no more character than the house next door - except what you can put into it yourself. If I can give you ideas about how to go about creating space and interest in your house, I will be content. Interior design is a long and fascinating study, and no book can capture in a few short pages all the difficulties. I have tried to keep the ideas simple and easily understood so that you can use them with confidence.

1. WHERE TO BEGIN

The eternal questions in interior design are: Where do I begin? What do I choose first? Do I pick the carpet and put all the other things with it? Or perhaps I should choose the curtains and work from there? Professional designers actually start at the end, with a mental picture of how things will eventually look. They gradually build things into the picture and, through a programme of adding and subtracting patterns and colours, they develop the final picture which the client had in mind. But all this is for the expert. For the average person, however, it is not easy to visualise what the end results are going to be.

The starting point can vary greatly. It depends on whether you are redecorating a room or whether you are starting with an empty room. You may even be confronted with a completely empty house where there may be many rooms or areas to think about.

Make a list

Let's take the room you are redecorating first and see how to go about it. You are trying to design a pleasing room interior, so don't make it difficult for yourself by trying to remember everything, keeping it all in your head - even the professional can't do it that way. You should always put things down on paper so that you can stand back and take a look.

First, make a list of all the things you already have and can't change - the fireplace, the windows. What are you keeping? Has your carpet a few years left in it? Maybe the curtains are quite new. Take a note of anything you must keep, either because it is permanent or because you can't afford to change it. Remember, the more things you have to keep, the easier it will be to redecorate. It won't make it more difficult. In fact, it will make it less so, simply because it cuts down on your options.

❑❑❑❑
Collect Samples

Now, start collecting samples of all the things you already have, if possible. If you have a piece of the carpet left under the stairs, pull it out and cut a small piece off. Try to do the same with anything else - curtains, upholstery and so on. If you have a fireplace to contend with, try to match up the colour or colours on a paint chart. Cut out the nearest colour sample you can get. Maybe the colour of your curtains is similar to the colour of a dress in a magazine. If so, cut it out.

When you have collected samples of everything you want to keep, get out a large piece of paper and put your samples on it. Then you can start designing. You'll be surprised at just how helpful a planning chart can be. It helps to relate everything you have already, and makes it so much easier to add other things to it. You can also take it to the shops with you. Don't be afraid to ask for samples of the materials you are looking at. Take them home and see how they fit with your plan. Try not to decide in the shop. You will find the lighting and atmosphere can influence you, sometimes in the wrong direction. Don't be too influenced by the sales talk of the shop assistants, although they can be helpful at times. In the long run, it is your own decision. You're the one who will have to live with it!

❑❑❑❑
Take a good look

When you have your list and your chart, take a good look at the room itself - not just the things in it. Then ask yourself a few questions.

Is it a large or small room?
Is it high or low or just average?
Is it a dark or bright room?
Does it get the sun or is it a cold room?
Has it any special features?

What are you going to do there? If it is a living room, what do you mean by *living*? Is it a family living room, or will it be kept for special occasions, when visitors call or for entertaining? Maybe it's a bit of both. You may want to read or watch television or do your knitting. If so, is your lighting good enough or in the right place?

The answers to all these questions will guide you and help you make up your mind about the room you want. The next few chapters will show you how to do this.

Sometimes you will have a totally empty room to design, for example in a new home. The approach is much the same as for redecorating. But this time you gradually put down brand new samples on your piece of paper. Try not to make a positive decision about any one feature until you have ideas for all the others as well. Don't be afraid to change your mind as you go along, particularly if you can't find the pattern or colour you want. Just try to do it another way instead.

It is rather more difficult if you have a whole house to do. In this case, simply take each room at a time. But remember that one area leads off another and you will have to go through one colour scheme to get to the next - for example, you must go through the hall to get to most of the other rooms. You will therefore need some form of relationship. Perhaps the same carpet will create a common bond between the areas you are decorating.

❑❑❑❑
Patterns and Textures

A quick word on pattern - don't overdo it! Too much pattern can squash your room, making it difficult for you to relax there. It is best to use only one pattern to break up the flat appearance.

If you really want to use a second pattern, make sure it is much smaller and that it relates to the main pattern in some way. Make the general pattern shapes similar, or try to co-ordinate the colour. But make one pattern definitely dominate the other while at the same time relating to it. Never use more than two patterns in the same room.

Pattern is useful because it can disguise wear or accident marks. A patterned carpet is easier to keep clean than a plain one because the pattern absorbs the foot marks. So think of the use your room will get. Your biggest area of pattern will be the upholstery, the curtains or the carpet. You can make this area dominate or blend in with other colours.

Don't forget that a texture or colour mixture can be used confidently in most areas. It is not really a definite pattern and can still disguise wear marks.

Remember!

- Make a list of what you can't alter and have to live with.
- Start collecting samples of colours and patterns.
- Let the room tell you about its size, shape, lightness, darkness, use etc. This information will guide you in your choices of colours, texture and pattern.
- If you already have a strong pattern, try not to introduce another pattern. If necessary, use a texture or mixture. Best of all, use plain colours - these can create more space.
- Isolate your colours so that you have a better opportunity of appreciating them and matching them.

Before you start thinking about colours, read on ...

2. LOOKING AT COLOUR

Colour is very much a personal thing and should be accepted as such. I have no intention of suggesting what goes with what. But I do want to show you what happens when you use certain colours and what they will do for you and your room. They are basic ideas which can be developed and added to - by you, with your own personal taste.

The colour wheel can help to guide you towards the best kind of colours to use to solve the problems of your room. It is a guide only and should not dominate your ideas. It will help to give you some idea of what might happen to your room by using certain colours.

The Colour Wheel

Let's look at a simple colour wheel (Figure 1, colour plate) where all the frills have been cut away to make it as simple as possible. The three large discs - blue, red and yellow - are the *primary colours*. It is not possible to mix other colours together to get a primary colour. When you mix any two of the primaries together, you get the colour in between - the *secondary colours* shown by the smaller discs. For example, red and yellow (two primary colours) will give you orange (a secondary colour).

Light and Dark

Look carefully at where the colours are positioned. The wheel is divided into several segments, first by the solid horizontal solid line which splits it into light and dark colours. The lightest colours are above the line. Yellow is the brightest of them all and is at the top. This is why yellow is used for road signs because it is the brightest colour of all. The darker colours are below the line. Purple, being the darkest, is right at the bottom.

You can lighten any colour by adding white to make it a *tint*. This can make purple into quite a bright colour. But if you add the same amount of white to both the yellow and purple shown on the colour wheel, yellow will still be brighter and have the highest light reflection.

You can also add black to any of the colours to darken them and create a *tone* of the main colour. Once again, the same amount of black added to both yellow and purple will still make the purple darker.

Here, then, is a piece of useful information from the colour wheel which can be used and applied to any room. When you look at your room, you may find out that it has a small window and that it tends to be dark. To make it as bright as possible, yellow would be the best colour.

There are a vast number of yellows available to choose from, but the lighter and paler, the more light it will reflect. Of course white (which is not a colour at all) will reflect even more light than yellow. It can be most effective, although it is far more difficult to use properly than most people realise. White can look splendid, but it may also be very difficult to live with and relax in.

❏ ❏ ❏ ❏
Movement and Temperature

Look again at the colour wheel and find the diagonal dotted line. This divides the wheel into two further areas - movement and temperature. Movement is the way in which the colours tend to advance or recede. Red, orange and yellow - to the right of the line - tend to advance or come towards you. Blue, green and purple tend to recede or go away from you. Of course the colours themselves don't actually move, but they give the impression of being either further away or closer.

To illustrate this more fully, look at Figure 2 (colour plate). The red square on the left tends to come towards you - as if you were sitting on top of a pyramid. The blue square on the right goes away from you - as if you were looking into a well or a bucket. It is only the colours that create these impressions. If they were photographed in black and white, they would look exactly the same. This is what is meant by colour movement - the appearance a colour gives of coming towards you or going away.

Once again, your room can give you a clue about what colour type to use. If you have a small room, space can be created by using a receding colour such as blue. You can add the last two points together as well. If you have a room which is both small *and* dark, perhaps you should be thinking of green, the one colour that is common to both areas of the colour wheel. Green is a bright colour as well as a receding one.

❏❏❏❏
Temperature

The colour wheel can provide information about temperature as well. Red, orange and yellow to the right of the line tend to appear warm. Green, blue and purple to the left of the line appear cold. This does not mean that the colours actually feel warm or cold - they simply appear to suggest warmth or coldness. It is easy to understand why red is a warm colour. It looks like fire and we associate fire with warmth. Blue is a cold colour and we even have expressions such as 'blue with the cold' and 'blue ice' and so on.

So here is another useful tip which can be applied to your room. If it faces north, you would help matters by choosing a warm colour to the right of the line. This would suggest a soft yellow, peach or apricot. If your room is dark as well as cold, then you could be thinking about soft, warm, light, reflecting colours such as yellows. By doing this, you will go a long way towards overcoming the minor defects of your room and creating the desired effect.

Even with the help of the colour wheel, problems may begin to loom. Suppose you have a room which is dark *and* cold *and* small! Green may be suitable for making it appear lighter and bigger, but it won't help to make it appear warmer. You may find that you can solve two out of three of your problems with reference to the wheel but you can't solve everything.

This is where a few more ideas and a little more basic information will help. It is perfectly possible to create space in various ways apart from colour. We will take a look at doing just that in the next chapter.

Remember!

- Red, Orange and Yellow   Warm and advance.
- Blue, Green and Purple   Cold and recede.
- Yellow, Green and Orange Good light reflectors, because they all contain yellow, the brightest colour of all.
- Red, Blue and Purple   Contain no yellow and are dullest, purple having less light reflection than any other colour.

Just for the record — white and black, although both brightest and darkest, are not colours at all.

3. NOT AS IT SEEMS

It is possible to look at things and not see them properly. We may see something else instead, or something that isn't there at all. This is the fascinating realm of illusions. It is by means of illusions that we can create space and make things appear different from what they are.

Usually two things are needed to create an illusion - a foreground and a background. With something in front of the background, and between the two, confusion can be created so that it is difficult to know just what is there.

Creating a Background

Background alone can influence how we see something. Take size, for example. The tone of the background can make an object appear bigger or smaller. Figure 3 shows this clearly. Here we have two discs, one white on a black background and one black on a white background. If you thought that it was perfectly obvious that the white disc is much larger than the black one, you would be wrong. You have been fooled! In fact both discs are exactly the same size. It is only the background which creates the illusion that they are different. In fact, you have actually seen something - a difference in size - that is not there at all.

This trick can be used in design very successfully. If, for example, you inherit a fine-looking sofa, you may want it to appear as large as possible. Simply cover it with a light material and put it in front of a darker wall and it will appear larger than it is. You can, of course, make your sofa appear smaller by doing the reverse.

Even though the examples shown in Figure 3 are in black and white, the important thing to remember is that they are demonstrating dark on light or light on dark - it doesn't have to be black and white. A pale primrose disc will look bigger when on any deeper colour. So it is possible to alter the apparent size by changing the background. This is a most important illusion, one which will crop up time and time again in decoration.

▲ *Figure 3*

These two discs are the same size. In fact the white disc on the black background looks bigger than the black disc on the white background.

You can also alter the *tone* of the colour. Look at Figure 4 (colour plate). There are two samples of blue, one on a black background and one on a white background. The one on the black background certainly appears lighter than the one on the white background. But once again you are not seeing correctly what is there. Both blues are exactly the same, but the darker background gives the impression that the patch is lighter and the light background makes the patch appear darker. This is also a useful decorating tip. In fact it is critical when it comes to choosing colours, particularly paint colours.

Most paint colour samples are shown on a white background. They will therefore appear dark - darker than they will be when you have them on the wall - because they won't be influenced by the background. Sometimes it is necessary to choose a lighter colour from the card than you need in order to get the exact colour you are looking for when it goes on the walls.

The background can also affect colour and cause problems. Take a look at Figure 5 (colour plate). Once again the two patches of colour, red this time, are the same. But they certainly don't look like it. The red on the yellow background looks purple, while the red on the blue background looks more orange. This apparent change is entirely due to the background. Have you ever tried to match up a piece of material, say a tweed, which has several colours in it? It's not as easy as it seems. If you take one of the strands to the local shop and match it up with _____ se, the odds are that it won't match up with _____ ou get home. The colour you chose may be _____ of the strand, but when the strand is part of _____ l, it can change dramatically. To get a match, _____ g the entire piece of tweed to the shop and _____ goes with it as a whole, and not as an

_____ to tell just how colours are going to react _____ ther colours. This is possible by going back _____ back to Figure 1 and take another look. If _____ lace it on one of the backgrounds - say blue _____ d to take on an orange tint, the tint of the _____ *site* it across the colour wheel. Orange is _____ en is opposite red, and purple is opposite _____ d patch in Figure 5 took on the appearances _____ rs know this. If they are asked to paint a _____ of a blue wall, they will automatically put _____ the grey to prevent it from looking orange.

❑❑❑❑

Introducing a Pattern

So here are three ways of altering appearances — size, tone or colour. But there are many other ways of achieving similar results. Size, for example, can be altered in ways other than changing the background. We have already seen how receding colours can increase space. But other things can also have a bearing. Pattern is a most useful asset to have up your sleeve. It can be introduced to re-shape your room as long as a little caution is used.

Stripes are an obvious way of increasing the height of a room, a fact which is almost too obvious to mention. Perhaps it is not so obvious, however, that wall-paper does not always have to hang up and down in vertical panels. It can also be hung sideways or even diagonally - extraordinary effects can be achieved with just a little imagination!

Stripes can so easily be placed horizontally instead of vertically. Additional width can be created in this way. Not all papers can be hung like this, but you are sure to discover some that can be used more adventurously. Very broad stripes can even be achieved by using two different coloured papers and hanging them alternatively. Do be careful, though. It may be perfectly possible to create space by such means. But it does not mean that the room will look well - and it might even look terrible.

❑❑❑❑
Shape, Size and Illusion

Shape can also affect the size of your room. Your room is formed from walls, floor and ceiling. It is the relationship between these that is important and which can be used to create your own simple illusion. Figure 6 is a simple example.

In Figure 6 there are two rectangles, A and B. Although they are exactly the same width, their heights are different, and A is not as tall as B. Because of the relationship between height and width, rectangle

A   B

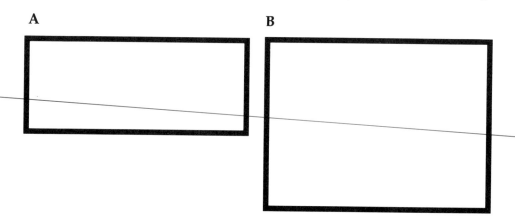

▲ *Figure 6*
The width of both rectangles is the same, but A looks wider than in B.

A appears wider than B. This example demonstrates how a room with a low ceiling can look wider than the same room with a high ceiling.

This is a most useful illusion to know about. Any room can be made to appear bigger by the simple means of colouring the ceiling to make it appear lower. This will tend to push out the walls as if by magic. Obviously it is only possible to use this if the ceiling is not too low to start with, but there are many rooms crying out for this kind of treatment. In the bathroom, or any other small room, the ceiling height will probably be the same as the height of the ceiling in the main bedroom or living room, although the room is only a quarter of its size. It makes sense to try to make the ceiling appear lower. This can be done with pure colour, although sometimes the use of a natural material such as Paraná pine sheeting can be most effective, adding warmth as well as making the room appear larger.

In older houses, rooms can be made to appear larger by adding picture rails. These are timber rails fixed to the walls about 18 to 24 inches below the ceiling. The wall colour is taken up to the level of this rail and then stopped. The ceiling colour is then taken on the wall above the picture rail. This will change the whole proportions of the room. The room will appear much larger because the eye is held at the picture rail and the ceiling height is apparently lowered.

Older houses sometimes have dados. The bottom two to three feet of the wall is panelled or papered and cut off from the remainder of the wall above with a rail, called the dado rail. If this dado is coloured in a tone of the wall colour, the height is reduced slightly and the area appears bigger.

There seems to be no end to the ways in which you can bring about changes in the size of your room. Here is yet another one. Look at Figure 7, where you will find a rectangle with its corners marked A, B, C and D. Which would you say is the longest line in this rectangle? Did you say either AB or CD? You'd be wrong, since the longest line is one you don't see at all - the diagonal AD or perhaps CB. This all sounds a bit geometrical, but it is a very useful bit of information. If you can express the diagonal lines in a room, such as in the pattern of the carpet, the lines will be as long as possible and will therefore tend to expand the room, since the eye is drawn along the length of the diagonal. This is most helpful in a narrow area such as a hall, where the diagonal lines will look longer than ones that are at right angles to the walls.

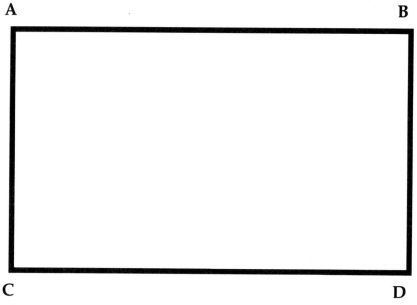

▲ *Figure 7*

In a rectangle, the longest line is the diagonal.

❑❑❑❑
Adding Width

When you have narrow rooms, or perhaps corridors or halls, a simple trick can help you to add width. Look at Figure 8 (colour plate) which shows areas marked A and B. Area A shows a simple narrow corridor with the same colour on each side. Because both side walls are close together, the eye sees them at the same time.

Look down any narrow corridor and close the right eye and you can see both side walls. Now open the right eye and close the left one, and you can still see both sides as before. In other words, your vision crosses, and you are seeing everything twice. This is why your hall will appear to narrow if the same colour is used on each wall. If slightly different colours are placed on each wall, as in B, the walls will tend to push apart because they are different colours.

Do be careful not to use strongly contrasting colours on each side such as red and green because these will catch the eye and hold it. Try to use two colours that are near to each other, such as pale blue and pale grey. This will give you the best results. The blue is also a receding colour and will tend to push out anyway. In this way you are using two ideas to help increase the width of your hall.

Take a look around any room and you will notice, if you look carefully enough, that the walls are slightly different shades although in fact they may all be the same colour. Because of the positions they are in, natural shadows may alter their tones somewhat. Walls in recesses, for example, may appear deeper in shade than walls in full light. This can also be used to create even more space and gain those extra few inches which make all the difference. Areas that are further away from you can appear deeper. If you use this idea you can create extra depth. Walls in the recesses on each side of the chimney breast, if painted a deeper tone of the main wall colour, can appear as if they are further away. You should be trying to suggest shade, and this will not work if you change the colour completely. Simply use a deeper tone of the same colour. You should hardly be aware of the change and with modern paint tinting machines in most large hardware shops, it is very easy to achieve this slight variation.

Remember!

- Size can be altered by the tone and depth of the background.
- Tone can be altered by the depth of the background.
- Colour can be altered by the colour of the background.
- Height will affect the size of your room.
- The diagonal is the longest line in your room.
- Opposite walls in the same colour in a narrow area can make it appear narrower.
- Shaded walls appear further away from the eye.

Any of these ideas will not actually make your rooms bigger, but they can certainly give the impression that they are bigger.

4. LIGIIT

When it comes to your home, there are really two kinds of light - natural and artificial. We will take a look at both of these to see how we can use them and how they will affect us.

Natural Light

Let's look at natural light first. This, of course, is ordinary daylight. But don't fool yourself - it is not all as simple as it looks. The way your room is facing can be of help. It can affect the way your colours look because colours change due to many things. Just try this little experiment and you will see what I mean. Put a sheet of white paper on a table in front of the window. Take a large book with a strongly-coloured cover, say red, and place one edge of the book along one edge of your white paper, the one furthest away from the window. Then tilt the book towards the window. You will see the white paper taking on a tint of the book cover. Figure 9 shows you what I mean.

This experiment shows you how ordinary light can take up the tint of another nearby colour and alter it. The book cover absorbs the daylight and reflects another colour back onto the paper.

Try this out in front of a mirror on your own face. Hold a piece of strongly-coloured paper under your chin and let the light bounce off it onto your face. You will see immediately what that colour can do for your complexion. This can be a great asset when it comes to choosing the colours of clothes for yourself - and it can prevent you from making disastrous mistakes.

Let's go back to your room again. If it faces out onto a large grass lawn, or if it is beside a projecting brick outside wall, the light reflected from those surfaces can alter any colour you may choose for the inside of your room, particularly if your choice is a pale pastel shade. So do be careful. In exactly the same way, the ceiling will reflect light down into your room. If the ceiling is in a strong colour it will affect your walls and the results could be most unfortunate.

There are many very soft tints around these days, sometimes called 'a hint of a tint'. These are so pale that if you get tinted daylight onto them as I have described, it could destroy their whole effect. Don't forget that any strong wall colour can pick up the daylight streaming through the window and can alter the colour of other walls by reflection. This can be particularly unfortunate if you use some of the strong feature wall colours which are so fashionable.

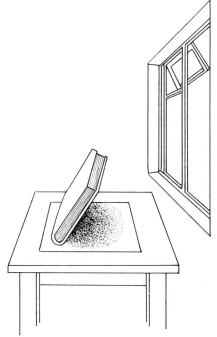

▲ *Figure 9*

Light coming through a window can borrow light from the object it strikes.

□□□□
Different Kinds of Daylight

Of course we have been looking at normal daylight only, while in fact there are different types of 'ordinary' daylight. If you visit your local art gallery, you will notice this - generations of artists have been aware of it.

In the morning at sunrise, the light is cool and thin, while in the evening it is rich and warm. The midday sun is halfway between the two. The same scene painted at sunrise would be quite different from one painted at sunset. If you go back to the room you want to decorate, the light could well vary, depending on which way the windows face. If the room faces east, it will catch the pale, cool morning sunlight. If it faces west, it will get all the warmth and richness of the setting sun. This could be very important in influencing the type of colours you should use. This variation in the sunlight will, of course, also be affected by reflecting off outside surfaces such as grass or brick as suggested above.

This may sound very complicated, and I suppose it is. But the best way to choose your colours is to do so in the room itself. Then you can see for yourself if there are any changes due to outside influences and aspect. Do be sure that you have a big enough colour sample. You just cannot expect the same results from a sample 1 inch square as you would from one 3 feet square.

🗖🗖🗖🗖
Artificial Light

Artificial light in the home is as important as the colours you actually choose. After all, colour is light. Without it, you would see no colour at all. I have shown you how natural light can alter due to circumstances. And of course artificial light also has its own problems.

There are many types of light bulbs, each giving out its own type and strength of light. Normal, standard light bulb types are available in most hardware shops and will fit the ordinary domestic type of fitting. All these bulbs have their own specific wattage - the amount of light they will give out. They can range from 25 to about 400 watt. Many of them come in either clear or pearl. There are also low voltage lamps which can be very economical to run, but these will also need their own transformers. If you are putting several of them in, it is possible to run up to four off the one transformer.

In domestic work, it is not very helpful to determine the amount of light you need for any room. This can be done by means of special calculations but on the whole it is unnecessary and tends to take any drama or excitement from the room. It is far better to make sure you have light where you need it. If you use dimmer switches instead of the normal rocker switches, the amount of light can be altered simply. It means that you can brighten or darken the amount of light you have available. This can only be done on tungsten lamps and will not work on either fluorescent or low voltage lamps.

You need to know what you will be doing in any room so that you can place lights where you need them most. If you want to read or sew, you need good direct light, but only in a small area - otherwise the whole room will be too bright. Don't try to carry out all your activities by means of the one, solitary central light fitting. In fact, in most of the rooms in ordinary houses, the central light could well be dispensed with entirely. It only breaks up a room and makes it appear smaller. It is generally far better to have one of the wall sockets switched on from the door so that when you come in you can immediately turn on a table or standard light or perhaps even wall brackets.

Most rooms look better without a central light. It is quite extraordinary what a difference its removal will do for a room. Do try to have enough wall sockets well spaced around the room so that you have places to plug in light fittings if you need them. This gives you greater flexibility, allowing you to move the furniture around more readily, and the light positions do not dictate layout.

❏❏❏❏
Lighting Effects and Fittings

Do you remember from an earlier chapter how the diagonal line can create space? This works with lighting as well. If you have a low table lamp on one side of the room with a high standard light on the other, you have created a diagonal line of light which will be longer than the width of the room and which will give you more apparent space.

Figure 10A (colour plate) shows a simple empty living room. Figure 10B shows what happens with a central light fitting. It shows the full height of the room and does not get the best from the room. Figure 10C creates a horizontal band using wall brackets. This cuts down the overall height of the room and makes it appear larger.

Figure 10D gives you an idea of what happens with the low table lamp on one side and the tall standard lamp on the other. This creates a diagonal 'sausage' of light, giving you that fraction more space.

Let's take a look at some of the types of fittings that are available and which we can use to create atmosphere and interest. This will help us to see how and when we should use each of them. Don't forget, any fitting should be properly checked to see what is the *maximum* wattage bulb that can be used in it. If you use a bigger bulb than stated on the fitting, it can blow the bulb. It can also be most dangerous and even melt the fitting itself.

❑❑❑❑
Direct Light

This is the strongest of all the types of artificial light and the source or bulb is actually exposed. On the whole it is uncomfortable to be able to see the bulb in this way. It must be screened from the eye, while at the same time directing the light onto the object we want to illuminate.

The obvious type of direct light that immediately springs to mind is the *anglepoise*, which can be turned and pointed in any direction. This is an extremely useful lamp for any home and is most suitable for when we are reading, knitting or doing any type of close work. It is the book we are reading or the work we are doing that is illuminated - not us. The light is therefore not in our eyes and so strain is eliminated.

Another type of fitting giving direct light is the *downlighter* which is concealed in the ceiling. The light source is not seen, but the light itself is projected downwards to give light where needed. Downlighters have many uses, and although people think of them as a commercial-type light fitting, this is far from the truth. They are very helpful to light areas difficult to reach by either wall or standard or table lights. Around the central area of a room, it is often advantageous to have light over the settee for reading without having to carry across a standard lamp with all its trailing wires. Carefully positioned downlighters can make excellent reading lights in this way. They are also very effective in kitchens, bathrooms and halls.

Another form of downlighter is the *eyeball fitting*. This is very similar to the last one, but it is possible to direct the light in any direction. An eyeball in the living room ceiling will still light up a dark area, even if the furniture is moved, because the light beam can be re-directed to the new position. For this reason eyeball fittings tend to give greater flexibility.

Track lights have become very popular. If used with discretion they can be most effective, even dramatic. A simple track is fitted to the ceiling and wired up. Various types of fittings can then be simply attached to the track at any point and pointed in any direction. The track is usually about four feet long and will take up to four lights which do not have to be the same. There are spotlights to illuminate a special effect or a picture, floodlights which will light up a large area - even what are called barn door fittings. These can control the size of the aperture for the light to come through by means of hinged shutters which look, for all the world, like four barn doors. This can be most useful to spotlight a particular object, and nothing else, because the light beam can be directed and controlled in size.

The final form of direct light is the *solid shade* type. This is very simple and is often found hanging at a low level over a table, for example. The light source is covered by the shade exactly as with the anglepoise. This time, you have no flexibility and it is only possible sometimes to raise or lower the shade.

❑❑❑❑
Indirect Light

This form of light gives less light than direct light, but it is more flexible and is easier to live with. A good proportion of the light is lost because it is reflected from another surface, and much depends on that surface. The *reflector* can either be part of the light fitting itself, or it can be a wall or other surface. The texture and colour of this will greatly affect the quantity and quality of your light. This type of fitting can be used for general light or what I call 'walking-about light' which is good enough for living in but not good enough for working with. Obviously the living room needs good general light for relaxing, for which indirect fittings are excellent. Softness and richness can be achieved by bouncing light from a wall or ceiling, and there are many types of fittings to do this.

❑❑❑❑
Diffused Light

In these fittings the light is pushed through a diffuser such as glass, plastic, vellum or fabric. The old-fashioned shade gives this form of light and the quantity and quality will depend on the shade itself. They can be made to appear either modern or old-fashioned. Old oil lamp type fittings are often used with diffused glass shades to give an old theme. Once again, visit your local showroom. Fabric shades can be made up as special orders from most materials. You can often supply your own material which can match up with your curtains or bedspread, for example.

❑❑❑❑
Composite Light

This is where you may have to use several types of lighting at the same time. In a living room, for example, you would need soft, relaxing light and would perhaps use indirect or diffused fittings. But if you also wanted to read or sew or do a detailed hobby, you would also need controlled direct light so that you could see what you were doing. These can sometimes be used off electric sockets like anglepoise lamps or can be fixed, as with downlighters.

❑❑❑❑
Concealed Light

You can conceal many types of lights, but normally it is done with fluorescent strips or spots or floods. When hidden behind a pelmet or baffle, these can give great effect. The curtain pelmet will hide the strip light and prevent it from being seen. Light is thrown down across the face of the material, giving richness and softness, and this is what is seen. Concealed light is simply a matter of hiding the fitting so that only the light is seen. Do remember that certain pelmets can sometimes be seen from the outside of the house and can look terrible if badly positioned.

Remember!

- Natural light isn't always pure daylight. It can be tinted by adjoining reflective surfaces.
- The walls in a room are different tints of the same colour due to their position.
- There are many different types of bulbs available.
- There are five types of lighting that you can use to create your interior:

  Direct light   Composite light   Indirect light

  Diffused light   Concealed light

5. WINDOW DRESSING

Few things make a room more bleak than an undressed window, one without curtains. It makes the room look unfurnished or Spartan. A soft curtain can do wonders to complete it. There are many ways to dress your windows, many materials that you can use and many ways of using them. Let us take a look at a simple window first. This is an average window with no trimmings and is shown in Figure 11A.

Dressing Things Up

There are one or two small points that are worth mentioning. When you have enough room, try to keep the sides of the curtain back from the edges of the window so that you get the maximum of daylight coming into your room. This is a generalisation, of course, and it is perfectly permissible to encroach on the window opening with your curtains. But on the whole you should have large windows for this to prevent the room appearing too dark.

In the evening, when you have the curtains drawn, does the light still penetrate through them? Use a blackout lining, which will blot out light penetration. A similar lining on all your curtains, especially on the front of the house, can make all your curtains look the same from the outside and give unity to your home.

One difficult decision to make is the length of your curtains - should they go to the floor or stop at the window board? If you have a radiator under the window, it is generally better to try and stop at the top of this. Otherwise all your heat goes up behind the curtain.

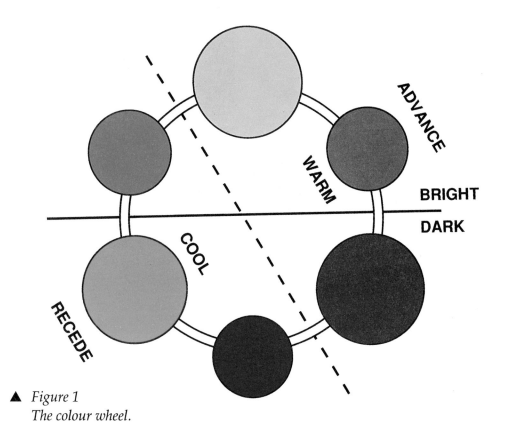

ADVANCE

WARM

BRIGHT

DARK

COOL

RECEDE

▲ Figure 1
The colour wheel.

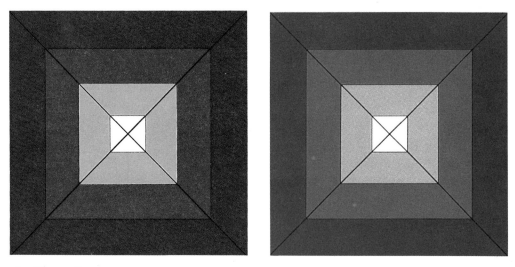

▲ Figure 2
Reds advance towards you while blues recede.

▲ *Figure 4*
These two colour samples are exactly the same. But the one against the dark background looks paler than the one against the light background.

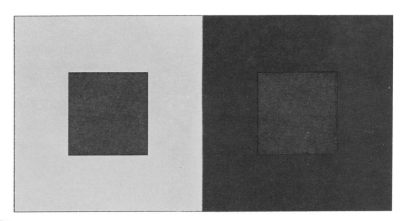

▲ *Figure 5*
The two samples of red are the same. The one against the yellow background looks more purple, while the one against the blue background looks more orange.

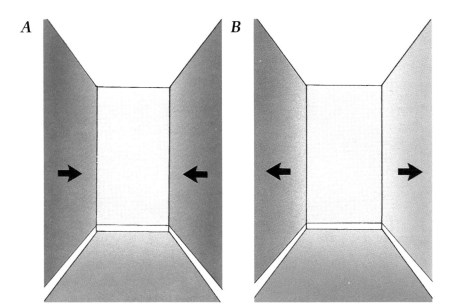

▲ *Figure 8*
When the same colour is used on both sides of a narrow corridor, it
becomes narrower than when two different but related colours are used.

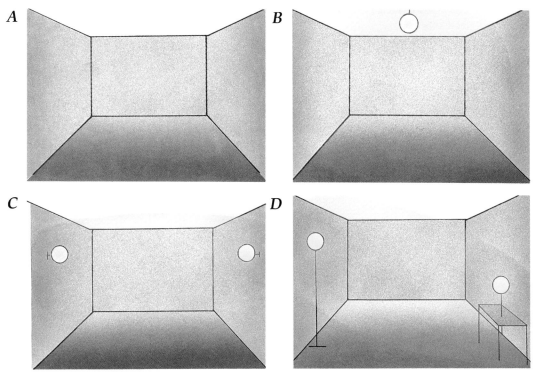

▲ *Figure 10*
Using light to create space.

A

B

▲ *Figure 12*
Tonal variations on windows.

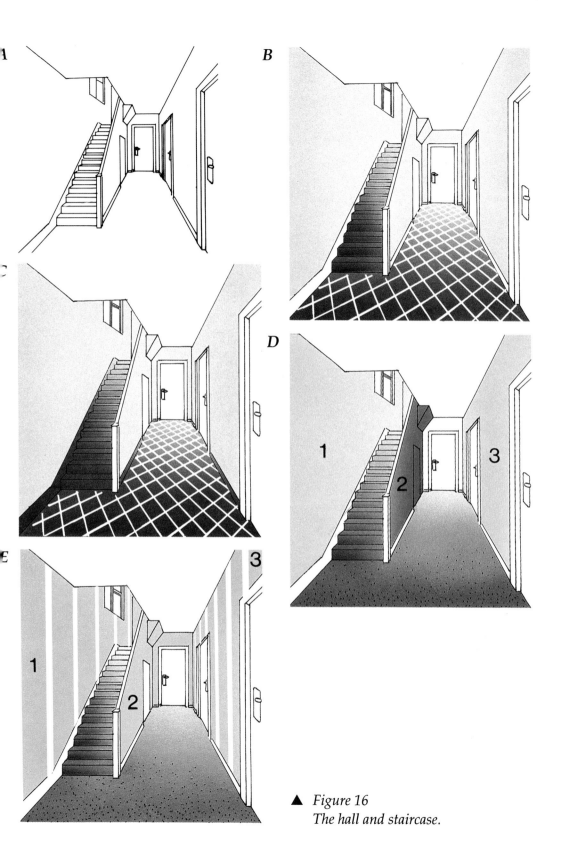

A

B

C

D

1 2 3

E

1 2 3

▲ Figure 16
The hall and staircase.

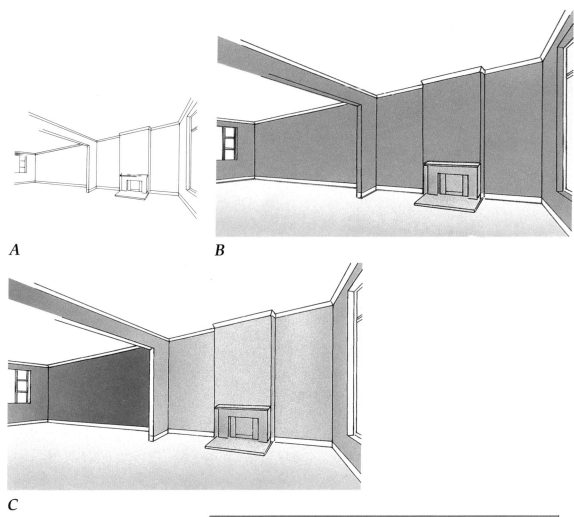

A

B

C

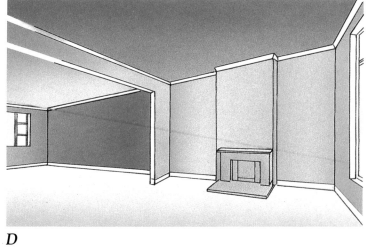

D

▲ *Figure 17*
The combined living-dining room.

▲ Figure 18
A well designed living-dining area.

▲ *Figure 24*
The melamine kitchen (Arco Kitchens).

There is no doubt that windows look better when dressed to the floor, but this is not always possible. If you do use a short curtain, try not to make it too strong in pattern or colour. Otherwise it appears to be sawn off at the bottom and it gets too much attention. If you use a curtain that is not too different from the walls, it will not stand out too much and will look much better.

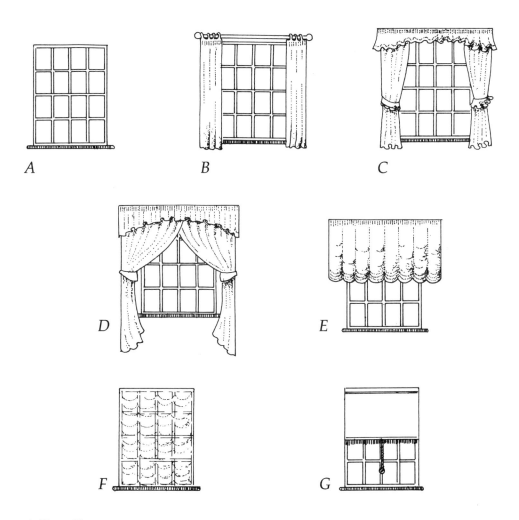

▲ *Figure 11*
Window dressings

Figure 11A shows the simplest window. In this case it is about 4' wide and 6' high and is 18" above the floor. Let us just see some different ways in which we can dress it to make it look better.

Figure 11B is possibly the simplest form of curtain. It is just a pull-type curtain gathered onto rings which slide along a pole. With a simple pole, it is not easy to fix cord pulls, but there are special poles made for this which work well. They are more expensive, but they give you the same appearance. Another thing to watch is that the pattern should match across the curtain. This is why they give you the measurement of the pattern repeat when you buy the material. Allowance should be made for this. Nothing looks worse than a curtain hanging up where the pattern is not straight across the window.

This type of curtain can be dressed up a little by providing a valance or pelmet at the top. This hides the top edge of the curtain and can be made from timber or the material itself. When in the same material, it can be pleated or draped into many types which we will look at later. Figures 11C shows what I mean. It is just a simple curtain which pulls to the side and has a material valance. The bottom edge of the valance can be finished with a decorative tape or with tassels or bobbles. It is an easy type of curtain to open with cords and there are many types of tracks available.

It is not always necessary to have curtains that draw back, and more dramatic ones can be used which drape or fall closed. Figure 11D shows the type I mean. The curtains are fixed at the top and do not draw along a track at all. To open them they are simply draped back and held with cords or behind hooks and they just fall back to a closed position. The main difficulty about these is that they do tend to block out light because they have to cross in the centre and you cannot draw them beyond the edges of the window opening. They can also be used with or without a valance, but a draped valance can be most effective. The one shown is simple and yet decorative. On the whole, these curtains should always be full length, down to the floor. The long sweep of the curved edges is lost when they stop at sill level.

Curtains do not have to draw back and there is yet another way of drawing them. The Austrian blind (Figures 11E) is such a type. It is fixed at the top and the blind is raised by means of cords. This time, however, it doesn't pull them apart but pulls them up into rucks or swags so that the curtain is stacked when open at the top of the window. This is a most popular type and is very much in vogue at the moment. This one has no pelmet or valance but this can be used if needed. You will notice that the curtain is generally larger than the window itself and this gives fullness and richness. However it can be made to fit into the window opening itself and Figure 11F shows this clearly. This type is perhaps best used with other curtains and can even be used with lighter materials such as net or sheers.

If you want something more economical, an ordinary roller blind is still a good choice. But of course it will not look as full or expensive as your curtain. Figure 11G shows how it fits into the window opening. It can be used effectively with other curtains. Don't forget that the bottom edge can be finished in many ways and can have frills, borders, fringes, brass rods etc. Another economical type of blind is the venetian blind which comes in various shapes. The ordinary horizontal type can have either narrow or wide blades. Whichever type you get, they do attract the dust and are hard to keep clean. They have the advantage that you can control your light coming into the room and can still get brightness without direct glare. The vertical blind is another form which can be very effective. The blades are much wider and are usually made up from material rather than from aluminium. They do not attract the dust so easily and you still have a certain degree of light control.

When you choose your curtains, don't forget the type of effect you are trying to achieve. You will remember our illusion of the black and white discs (Figure 3). This showed how light on dark looked bigger than dark on light. If you want your window to look as big and as full as possible, it is best to have your curtains lighter than your walls. This will do the trick. Just look at the difference between Figure 12A and Figure 12B (colour plate). You can see for yourself how one appears bigger than the other, although they are both the same size.

So far we have just looked at some of the normal simple types of drapes or blinds. But of course we can mix them and use them in combinations. Figure 13 shows just two of the many that are available to you.

A   B

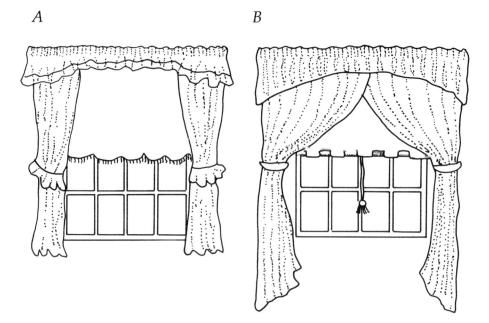

▲ *Figure 13*
Combination curtains

Figure 13A shows the draw type with a pleated valance. This time there is an Austrian blind set into the window frame behind. This blind can be in a sheer or light material. It can be drawn on its own and in the dark evenings both sets of curtains can be drawn across. The whole thing looks that little bit more expensive, which it is. Figure 13B shows the draped curtain. This time there is a roller blind set into the window frame. There is no limit to the variations you can create.

❏❏❏❏
Pelmets and Valances

We have talked about the pelmet or valance, so perhaps this is the time to take a more careful look at them. Figure 14 gives you an idea of the many forms that your pelmet can take. They can be in many different materials, but I have shown them in a material which should be the same as the curtains themselves.

'A' is a *simple pleated pelmet*. The pleating should be the same as that used on the curtains themselves.

'B' is a *swagged curtain*. The material is draped from the two corners to overlap at the centre. It gives a nice finish to the bottom edge which can be decorated with fringes or bobbles.

'C' is a wavy pelmet with a soft, long curve. This is also pleated along the top edge to give it a fuller effect.

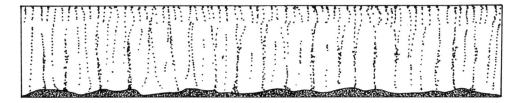

A

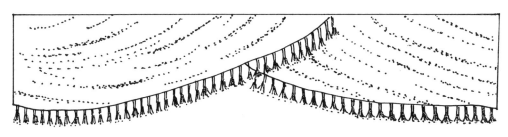

B

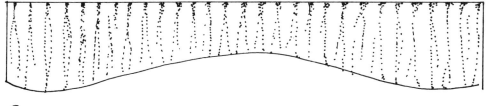

C

▲ *Figure 14*
Pelmets

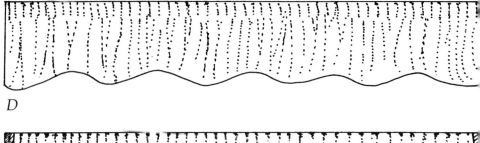

D

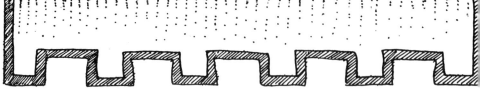

E

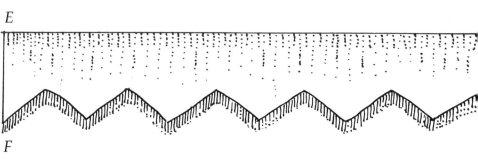

F

'D' is similar, but the waves are much smaller and the bottom is scalloped.

'E' is *castellated* and 'boxed' along the bottom edge, somewhat like the top of a castle wall. Sometimes this is trimmed with a border material to finish it off.

'F' is pointed and is very simple. A fringe along the bottom edge gives a good soft effect.

Of course there are other types of pelmets, but these are the most popular ones. They are quite simple to make. They can also be manufactured from wood and painted, but the material ones look the most expensive.

❑❑❑❑
Pleats

It can often mystify people as to what to do with the top edge of the curtain - what type of pleating is best.

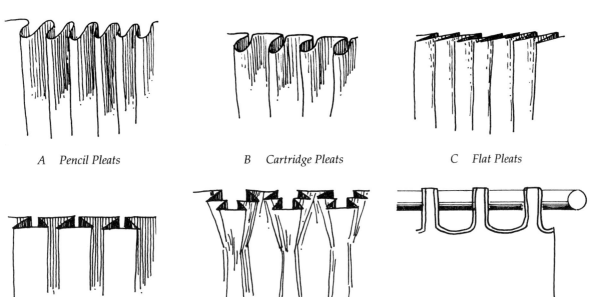

A   Pencil Pleats   B   Cartridge Pleats   C   Flat Pleats

D   Box Pleats   E   French Pleats   F   Scalloped Pleats

▲ *Figure 15*
Types of pleats

There are many types and the following are just a few.

Pencil pleats (Figure 15A) are small folds drawn along the top of the curtain using a Rufflette tape. They are small and effective and are best used for small homely curtains of a light material such as cotton.

Cartridge pleats (Figure 15B) are larger and fuller. They are pinched in at the back of the pleat to form little barrels. These are better used with heavier materials

Flat pleats (Figure 15C) look like what they sound like. Your material must be fairly fine and not too bulky.

Box pleats (Figure 15D) give a good appearance and really are double pleats flattened out. They are somewhat sophisticated.

French pleats (Figure 15E) are excellent for large areas of curtain. They help to divide the long spaces out into bunches of pleats. They are waisted just below the top of the curtain.

Whatever type of pleating, Rufflette make a tape that will give you the effect you are looking for. Once it is stitched to the top of the curtain, you just draw the cords. Then, as if by magic, you get the type of pleating that is shown on the front of the box!

Sometimes the curtain is fixed directly to a pole with rings, and no pelmet. This can be done simply by sewing the top edge to the rings. A tape can be used for this purpose, with hooks set in and then fixed to the rings.

A final type of curtain top is somewhat limiting because it is almost impossible to draw. This is the *scalloped heading* which has a series of loops formed along the top edge with the pole threaded through them as in Figure 15F. This is very good for half curtains - those that do not go up to the top of the window, but start half way up instead.

The curtains are an important feature in your room and deserve a little thought. But be careful that this thought does not stop with the choosing of the material itself. That little extra bit of care will show and will make all the difference in the world.

Remember!

- Keep your curtains back from the sides of the window to get maximum light.
- Full length curtains draw the heat up behind them when in front of a radiator.
- If your curtains are very light, you may need heavy lining material to stop light coming through.
- Draped curtains can block out daylight.
- Use a curtain heading that is suitable for the weight of your material and the size of your window.
- Remember what light curtains against a dark wall will do for your window.
- Choose your pelmet to suit your curtain material.
- Rufflette tape will shape all your headings like magic.
- Go to your local showroom and see what is available.

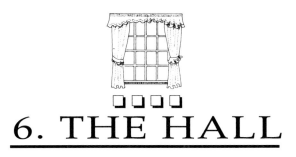

🗆🗆🗆🗆
6. THE HALL

🗆🗆🗆🗆
First impressions

When starting to decorate your home, there is no better place to begin than in the hall. This is the first place a visitor sees, so you have an opportunity of creating a wonderful impression of what the remainder of your house is going to look like.

Most halls are fairly small and tight and space is a problem. At the same time, you usually spend very little time in the hall, simply passing through it to get to the other rooms. This 'passing through' can cause certain difficulties because all the other rooms radiate off it and are first seen from the hall when we open the various doors. It is therefore essential to have some form of unity between the hall and each of the rooms so that one doesn't scream out against the other.

If you look at the problem in depth, you will realise that it is far better to have a completely different type of scheme in the hall than anywhere else. This is most helpful from a living point of view, and good strength of colour or some form of visual cut-off is excellent. This actually gives the eye a jolt as you go from room to room. It is a form of psychological equivalent to washing one's face to freshen up. For example, if you are in a soft, relaxing room such as the living room, you will pass through the hall to get to another room, say a bedroom, which is also relaxing. If the hall is strong and vibrant, there is a brief stimulation of the mind, that washing of the face to freshen up that we just talked about, which occurs between the two areas of relaxation in the living room and the bedroom.

This stimulation is good in the hall because you don't spend much time there. It can also be most welcoming for arriving guests. The amount of excitement you generate is all controlled by personal taste, so it is up to the individual to decide how far to go.

❑❑❑❑
Design Choices

Some people prefer a form of neutral scheme in the hall so that all the rooms off it won't clash. This works well, although it hasn't got the same excitement or impact.

No matter what type of scheme you go for, let the hall talk to you and give you ideas. Figure 16A (colour plate) is an illustration of a simple standard hall in a typical semi-detached house. It is probably just like your own home and like the house next door and like the ones down through the estate, with only minor modifications. The main difference between yours and everyone elses is that this is *your* home - it is you that makes the difference, not the hall. This means that you should put something of yourself into decorating it.

With such a narrow area, it is well worth while trying to make it appear wider and bigger. This can be achieved in many ways. Let's start with the carpet, for no other reason than that we have to start somewhere and this is probably the most expensive thing that will be going into your hall. Remember Figure 7 which showed how to use the diagonal to create space. This can be very useful for your hall. Figure 16B shows how a diagonal pattern can spread out the narrow part of your hall. The eye travels along the diagonal line and adds width because the line is actually longer.

It is not necessary to have the staircase carpet the same unless you want it that way, but it should always at least be related in some way. A good relationship can be achieved by having a patterned carpet in the hall and a plain carpet, with the same colour as the background of the patterned one, on the stairs. This will do one thing for you. It will make your stairs safer because you will be able to see where your stairs start and finish more readily. Some patterns, when used on stairs, can actually distort the stairs' appearance, making them appear curved or sloping. So if you do use any pattern on the stairs, be sure to try it out first to see how it looks. A standard sample length would probably be large enough to do this and it is well worth all the extra trouble.

A very simple and effective way of increasing the width of your hall is to paint the skirting in a similar colour to the carpet. It will then be difficult to know where one starts and the other finishes. It can give the appearance of adding another 4 to 6 inches to your hall. Figure 16C shows how this works. The eye no longer stops at the carpet edge, but drifts up on to the skirting and adds those extra helpful inches. If you are trying to match up with a patterned carpet, try to match the background. You will also find that if you can get an exact match, the skirting will appear lighter because it has not got the texture of the carpet to add depth. So do try to get a colour that is a few shades darker where you can. Modern paint machines give you an excellent chance of obtaining most of the colours you will ever need, and they are now installed in most of the larger hardware stores.

The walls come next on the list. How do you get that little bit of extra space that makes your hall look bigger than someone else's down the road? Figure 8 showed how your vision crossed, causing you to see both sides of the hallway at the same time. You can now use this idea to create the space you were looking for, although you still need a little caution. Figure 16D shows how to go about it. If you colour the two walls furthest away from each other the same (1 and 3 on the sketch), and choose a different colour for wall 2, you will help the situation. What happens is that walls 2 and 3 are close together and will draw together if they are the same. So these two walls should be different. The eye will be drawn across wall 2 to wall 1 on the other side of the staircase. You can see how the eye is helped to travel right across the hall to give maximum effect.

The difference between the two colours you choose should not be too great. Don't use red on one and green on the other - otherwise you will break the whole thing up. Use two colours that are softly related, perhaps pale blue and pale grey. In this way you won't be really aware of the colour change and the effect will be even greater.

In Figure 16E you can see how a striped paper is used on walls 1 and 3 and a plain colour on the central staircase wall 2. With this technique, the eye is pulled across the full width of the area. Another trick is to carry the plain colour you used on wall 2 onto the small section of wall around the kitchen door at the end of the hall. Carry the colour around the corner, and this will tend to create even more space. It is also a good idea to use a similar colour in gloss on the kitchen door. This will give more of the colour and help to lose the kitchen door, which is not a bad idea in itself.

❏ ❏ ❏ ❏
Dressing it up

The doors themselves do not have to be all the same, although you should have some form of relationship. There is something to be said for having the doors different. If you look down your hall, you will notice one thing. The kitchen door at the end of the hall is at right angles to you. You can see the whole thing as soon as you come in through the hall door. The other doors to the dining room and living room on the side wall can only be seen at an oblique angle. Yet they are more important from the visitor's point of view. So it is logical that they should be stronger than the kitchen door to give them more impact. They could be in hardwood if you like, but do try to make all the frames and architraves around the doors in white on *all* doors so that you get your relationship. This architrave acts rather like a picture frame, and different pictures can be put together in a much better fashion if all the frames are identical.

Pictures can help to dress your hall but if you put them in the wrong places you can undo all you have been trying to achieve. Don't, for example, put them on wall 2, the one in the centre. This will only stop the eye and prevent it travelling on further. The best place for pictures is on the wall along the staircase to draw the eye across. Many people place pictures too high. Generally speaking, they should be placed so that the centre of the picture is at eye level. If you have several pictures of different sizes, you should not line up all the bottoms or the tops. Instead, you should line up the centres. This will make the tops and bottoms out of line but they will generally line up in a better fashion. If you want to, you can step pictures up the stairs so that they are all at different levels. I find it better to form a group of pictures at ground floor level or on the landing. Such a grouping can be made up from many small pictures kept about two inches apart at their edges. This creates a good effect and makes small pictures more attractive.

❏ ❏ ❏ ❏
Windows and Light

Most semi-detached houses have a small landing window looking out at the side onto the neighbour's house. It seems difficult for most people to know what to do with it. Whatever you do, don't put a strong curtain on it. This makes your eye dash up the stairs and makes this unimportant window far too noticeable. It should not be seen and is only meant to shed a little light onto your stairs. Try to keep it in a colour rather similar to your wall so that it dresses the window but disappears and does not show up too strongly.

It is surprising that many people accept the positions for lighting that the builder has fixed for them. They just hang a shade onto the flex from the ceiling and that would appear to be that. Much of the effect of your lighting can be lost if you do not give it a little thought. If you hang a shade from the ceiling point, it is often possible to see into the fitting when coming down the stairs. It does not always look very pretty. If you keep your lighting low, you can create more space. However, it is not always feasible or practical to do this in the hall, where there is a lot of traffic and children are running up and down the whole time and perhaps knocking fittings over. Perhaps the best compromise is to use downlighters. If these are fitted into the ceiling where the builder has allowed for hanging fittings, it can be done very economically and with great effect. The source of the light is almost lost and the light beam streams down onto the floors or stairs. You can also set an eyeball fitting into the ceiling. This could illuminate pictures and the light beam can be directed onto what you want. Picture lights are good, but they stick out from the wall a bit and can be knocked, especially if they are on the low side. If you can manage it, a low table lamp behind the hall door in the corner, facing the stairs, gives a rich effect to people coming in.

Remember!

- Little time is spent in the hall. You can make it bold or exciting.
- Other rooms are seen off the hall.
- Make it different from your rooms.
- Use the diagonal line to create space.
- Colour the skirting the same as your floor to add inches to the hall.
- Two different wall tones or papers can make the area bigger.
- All doors don't have to be the same.
- Be careful where you put pictures.
- Don't make the curtains on the landing window too strong.
- Be a little adventurous with your light fittings.

7. LIVING AND DINING ROOMS

There are several types of living room. You can have a relaxing room without distractions where you go to sit down and enjoy the television or listen to music. You can have a living room which is only used when there are visitors and which is always tidy ... or you can have a combination of both. You can also have the combined living and dining room, study room and so on. Every type of room should express what you want to use it for and be suitable for doing those things.

What should dominate?

Try to decide first and foremost on a dominant feature for your room. This usually is the fireplace and the entire room is built around that feature. All the furniture stands each side of it to get near the fire and to reinforce its importance.

Don't put strong colour around the fireplace because this can be a distraction and can draw the eye. Use soft, simple contrasts. Avoid strong contrasts of tone such as black and white, or dark brown and cream. This can become very disturbing as the eye travels from one to another, as shown in Chapter 3. Keep your level of lighting down and don't have it too bright. Have light where you want it for reading or sewing or close work, but confine it to those areas only. Don't be afraid to get rid of the centre light altogether. It is extraordinary what an effect this small item alone can create.

Give your room a good, even balance throughout. If you want to introduce strong colours, try to do so out of the line of normal vision - in other words behind you when you are sitting down.

The dining room is completely different and the object here is to eat. The dining table is the focal point and everything should lead towards this. Strong rich or deep colours can be used with effect on the walls which will act as a background to the table only. They can give a good sense of enclosure and cut you off from the cares and woes of the world as you eat your meal and talk to visitors or friends.

The light should be low over the table or on a pulley so that it can be lowered or raised. Try to keep other lighting out of the room as much as possible. A small table lamp may be necessary on a serving table, but do try to make the main table dominate. Curtains are best when they are as near the wall colour as possible so that they do not stand out.

❑❑❑❑
Living-dining Areas

There is always doubt as to what to do if you have a living-dining room, when both rooms are opening off one another. Do you paint them the same colour? Do you carry the carpet through? How can you relate both of them and yet get the different approaches that I mention above?

Figure 17A (colour plate) shows part of such a room, where there is a dividing wall which has a large opening cut in it and both rooms can be seen at the same time. There is a fireplace at one end only and it is obviously two rooms joined into one. They do not have to be the same. The different usages certainly point to the fact that they should be different. But the trick is to get them each with their own personality and yet related.

Figure 17B shows what the result would be if you put the same colour throughout. It's a bit monotonous and doesn't do a thing for the area. Figure 17C shows the same area again. But this time different colours are placed in each area. Although this can be interesting, it tends to break the area into two smaller parts and you loose apparent space.

One simple method of making things more professional, as if it was designed like this, is by using two simple colours, one a deeper tone than the other. This is shown in Figure 17D. If you choose your colour carefully, you should be able to get something relaxing in a pale tint which would go well in the living room end. Now try to select a colour which is similar but several shades darker and use this on the ceiling in the living area. It is always helpful if you have a small cove or cornice which should be in white to divide the two colours. Now you have a light shade on the wall and a darker one on the ceiling. If you reverse these two in the dining area and put the darker one on the walls and the lighter one on the ceiling, you have a complete relationship and yet a difference. You have the pale, light, warm tint in the relaxing area and the deeper, more confining one in the dining room. To draw the two further together, the same carpet colour throughout is useful, acting as a base for the entire scheme. You can now build up from this with furniture colours. These can be whatever you like, and you don't have to match up at all unless you want to. In the hall we tried to make the skirting the same general colour as the carpet. This will do just as much for the size of your living room and is well worth trying.

The photograph in Figure 18 (colour plate) shows what can be done with a small living-dining area.

❑ ❑ ❑ ❑
Curtains and Lights

When it comes to hanging curtains in these rooms, you will find that it is not essential to have them the same at each end. To start with, you cannot see both sets of curtains at the same time because they are so far apart. When you face one, you have your back to the other. With decoration of this nature, the curtains will be seen against different wall tones and can be chosen accordingly. It is always better to have something similar about them so that there is a general relationship, but they don't have to match exactly.

Lighting your rooms is most important and can do wonderful things for you. Once again, you should use two forms in each area. I find the best for the living area is in the form of standard and table lamps. If they are selected and placed with just a little care, you can develop a diagonal of light which will create more space. (Remember that we showed you how to do this in Chapter 4.) Don't forget what we have already said about colour tones. When you want a relaxing room, try to avoid strong tonal contrasts. If you have a sofa out in the centre of the room and you need to read while sitting on it, you will need good light. It is not always possible to carry a flex across the carpet without tripping over it. Don't forget the downlighter. This fits into the ceiling and can be placed wherever you like in the ceiling. If placed directly over the sofa, it will give excellent light. Because it is recessed, you do not tend to see it so much from the side as you would a hanging pendant and the line of the ceiling is not broken up. If you use an eyeball unit, you can adjust the beam of light to different positions. This is very useful if you move your furniture about.

The main lighting in the dining room should be over the table, preferably on a pulley. This will light that area only and everything else should disappear. It doesn't really matter if the dining room walls are not illuminated. What does matter is that the table and the faces of those sitting at it are well lit. Nothing else is of importance. This will create great atmosphere and be a complete contrast to the type of lighting that you used in the living room. A table lamp or picture light is all that is required on the serving table so that it is possible to see what you are doing. But do keep the bulb as small as possible.

It is excellent idea to have dimmer switches on all these lights. You can obtain good light variation in this way. The best type to use is the dimmer with an additional switch so that you do not alter the quantity of light each time you switch it on.

When it comes to hanging pictures or mirrors, do be careful. The living room section is the place to make them stand out. You can even put picture lights over them, providing they are good enough to light up, since there is no point in illuminating something that is not worthwhile. In the living room, the pictures can draw the eye to its fullest extent beyond the furniture. This can give you more space, as long as you don't go mad and have pictures everywhere. Use them to help to balance other things such as windows and doors and curtains, making the entire room well balanced and relaxed.

In the dining room the pictures are there to avoid emptiness. They should not take away or distract from the table area. They should be simple and small. Do not try to draw attention to them even if they are good.

Do not forget that these rooms in particular are the ones that express your personality to visitors more than any of the others. They will create an impression and tell guests just the kind of person you are. Don't think they don't notice - they do.

Remember!

- What is to dominate your rooms?
- Avoid strong tonal variations if you want to relax.
- In a living-dining room, both ends don't have to be the same, but they must relate.
- The lighting in the living area should be different from that in the dining area.
- Use diagonal lighting to create space.
- You will need light to read by as well as to move about in.
- Put your lights on dimmer switches if you can.
- Use your pictures to create space.
- Balance your room.

8. KITCHENS

The kitchen is probably one of the most difficult rooms in the house to design and it deserves a good deal of thought. Just decorating it is no real problem, but re-designing it has many difficulties. This is a room in which you spend a great deal of time, so every effort must be made to make sure that you get it right - or as right as possible anyway. You won't be able to solve all your problems, but you can make sure that you haven't created others that are even worse.

Layout is Essential

If you are putting in new fittings you must bear several things in mind. Don't worry about where your old fittings were. It is quite possible they have been in the wrong places for years. Try to get your circulation right. You will find that a proper layout with good circulation cuts out a great amount of running around, making it easier to carry out most tasks.

The relationship between the jobs you will be doing and the layout is essential. Let's look at a simple kitchen and see if we can lay it out successfully. Perhaps the simplest way is to try doing something like making a beef casserole. By doing this we will find how the units should be positioned. Figure 19 shows how we go about this.

First of all we must go to the fridge, get out the meat and vegetables and place them on a table area beside it. The fridge unit should therefore come first, with perhaps dry storage cupboards over it to house goods such as packet peas or fruit. A flat space beside the fridge is most useful. Not only can you place all your articles for your casserole on it; it is also very useful to put down your bags full of shopping before decanting them into the relevant cupboards or fridge.

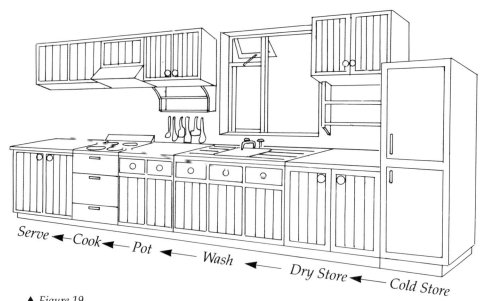

▲ *Figure 19*

The kitchen and its circulation

After taking everything out of the fridge, you will want to wash everything. So the sink unit should come next. If possible, try to get this under the window. This not only gives you good light, but also gives you a view over the garden, making your work more pleasant.

Once everything is washed, you will want to cut up and prepare your dish, so some flat countertop area comes next. Over this you would need your herbs and stock cubes placed on shelves or in a cupboard. Below the countertop would come your pot storage.

This leads naturally to cooking and to the cooker which should have a hood over it. Try to have a proper fan outlet leading from your hood to extract all steam and smell from the cooker. There are special filter units that eat up the smells, but I have never found these satisfactory. You can't go wrong if you have a length of pipe and a proper fan.

When you have finished cooking, you want to serve the meal. A serving counter is a great advantage beside the cooker, especially when there is one on each side.

When you have served, you then want to be near the eating area or table. This table should not be too far away from the sink unit so that plates can be scraped and rinsed before washing.

So here is the rough kitchen circulation that works well.

1. Fridge with dry storage above
2. Work top with vegetable storage below
3. Sink unit
4. Preparation table with pot storage under and herb space above
5. Cooker with hood and fan over
6. Serving

❑❑❑❑
Different Layout

We have shown this circulation all strung out in a straight line, but of course not all kitchens will take this kind of layout. There are basically four types of layout and Figure 20 shows them all.

The *Inline* kitchen (Figure 20A) is exactly as we show it above. All the fittings are along one wall.

The *Galley* (Figure 20B) has fittings on each side of the room. All the fittings are in the same order. If we follow the dotted line, we have exactly the same circulation. This layout will work with a short, wide kitchen but you should have enough room for the doors on your units to open and still be able to get past them.

The *L-Shaped* kitchen (Figure 20C) is where you carry your fittings around a corner on two walls that butt up together. Once again you have the same circulation and the dotted line shows how each unit follows the other in proper order. One of the problems with this kind of layout is that you have a dead corner marked with the letter X. Because each unit butts up against it, it is very difficult to store anything in and still be able to get it out again. But we'll offer some suggestions at a later stage.

The *U-Shaped* kitchen (Figure 20D) is much the same as the last. This time, your fittings go around three walls and you find yourself with two dead corners marked X.

Here then are the kinds of basic layout you should try to obtain. The shape and size of your kitchen will dictate the form it should take.

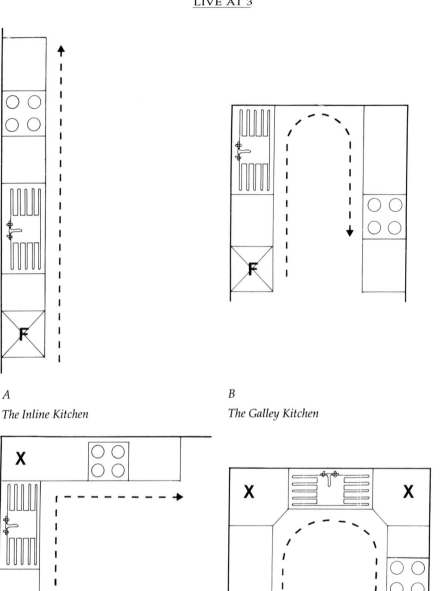

A

The Inline Kitchen

B

The Galley Kitchen

C

The L-Shaped Kitchen

D

The U-Shaped Kitchen

▲ Figure 20

Layouts for the Kitchen (F = fridge)

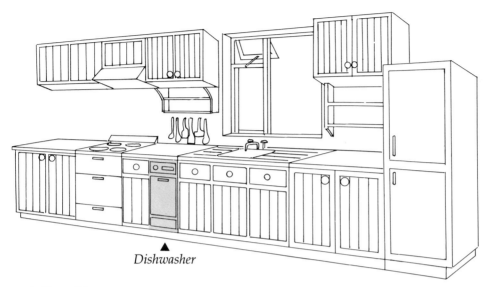

Dishwasher

▲ *Figure 21*

Fitting in the Dishwasher

Of course there will be problems such as where to put your dishwasher and how it will fit into the circulation. Figure 21 shows how this can be achieved without destroying your layout altogether. Because of the plumbing which is necessary, it is best to keep it near the sink. Either side of the sink unit would be all right, although, as you will be bringing dirty dishes back from the dining table, it is better that it should be placed on the cooker side of the sink unit. Another item which can make a mockery of your layout is the popular microwave oven. Where better to place it than beside the cooker, possibly on the serving counter.

❑❑❑❑
Good Gimmicks

There are also the little gimmicks that help to make kitchens so attractive and serviceable. You often find, for example, that the ends of units stop very suddenly and that they need some form of dressing to make them look like anything at all. This has all been thought of, and depends on how much you have to spend. You can simply have half-round open shelves which will take baskets or plants and which can look quite well. Sometimes these shelves can have little rails either in timber or brass running around the curve to stop things falling off. They can be most attractive, as Figure 22 illustrates.

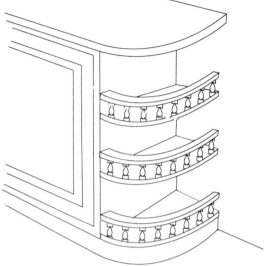

▲ *Figure 22*
Little things can give character to your fittings.

Another useful item is the pedal bin. But where do you put it with your new layout? It is perfectly possible to have it built in, usually under the sink. When you open the door, the lid of the bin pops open so that you can have both hands free for your scraping.

Then there are the dreaded areas marked 'X' on the sketches in Figure 20 — those parts of the cupboards in the corners that you can't get at. There are three ways of solving this problem and Figure 23 shows them all. 'A' shows the door open with a half-round carousel-type tray on the back which is exposed and comes out with the door swing. I must say I don't like this one myself. Things fall down the side and shelves bend. All in all, I have never found them satisfactory, although I am sure some people would disagree. Sketch 'B' shows an alternative where the front corner of the unit is splayed. There is a door across the splay which opens to allow you to get at the inside. This is simple and effective and you can just about get at the interior and into the corners. My own preference is for the special two-door corner unit in 'C'. Here, both doors open and expose far more of the interior. It is certainly easier to store things and get at them afterwards.

There are so many space-saving gadgets that the mind quite boggles! There are special deep food drawers, ironing boards built in, mixer shelves, tray shelves and so on. These items can add to the cost of your units, but most of them are effective. It really is a matter of shopping around to see what you can get and what you really want. Please, whatever you do, don't let these gadgets take preference over good layout. The circulation is the most important thing, while the others are just the icing on the cake.

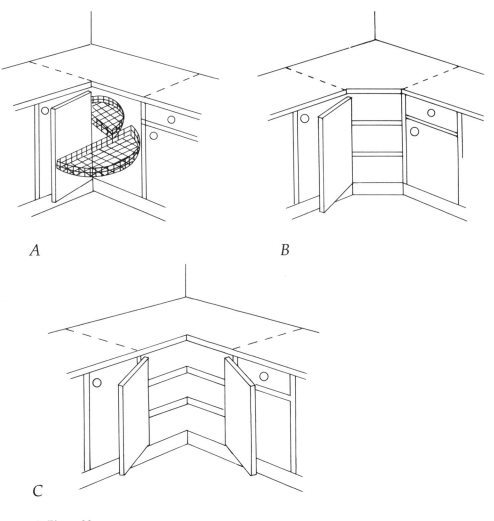

A

B

C

▲ *Figure 23*
Getting at things in the corner unit

❏❏❏❏
A Variety of Finishes

So far you have only been looking at the overall layout, but what about the actual look of the fittings themselves? There is a large range to choose from, depending on the money you have available. There are really only five different types, all with minor variations.

The melamine kitchen
The melamine kitchen with hardwood edge trims
The kitchen with light hardwood fittings
The kitchen with dark hardwood fittings
The unfitted kitchen

The first four are standard unit-type kitchens. They are available from most kitchen specialists and vary from company to company in price and standards. The melamine kitchen (Figure 24, colour plate) is the simplest form available. It is plastic faced and there are no tricks or frills. The cost is fairly basic and for low budget layouts, this is the one to go for. The look can be upgraded by fitting hardwood edges, trims and handles, as shown in Figure 25 (colour plate). It softens the look of the kitchen generally and looks that bit more expensive. Figure 26 (colour plate) is a light hardwood type layout and is going more up-market again. It gives good light reflection and is not too heavy and can be used effectively in fairly small kitchens. The dark wood kitchen in Figure 27 (colour plate) needs a good, bright room to achieve the best results and is better still if the room is reasonably large. This type cannot be cramped up too much.

The sketch in Figure 28 shows an unfitted kitchen. This is the purpose-built, specially-designed, one-off kitchen which is sought after by people who want something different and special. The best unfitted kitchens are not based on standard units lined around the walls. Every attempt is made to make them appear as if they have just happened rather than been designed. Make no mistake, they are the most expensive of them all, but you do get something nobody else has. You will positively have to employ a specialist designer for this type.

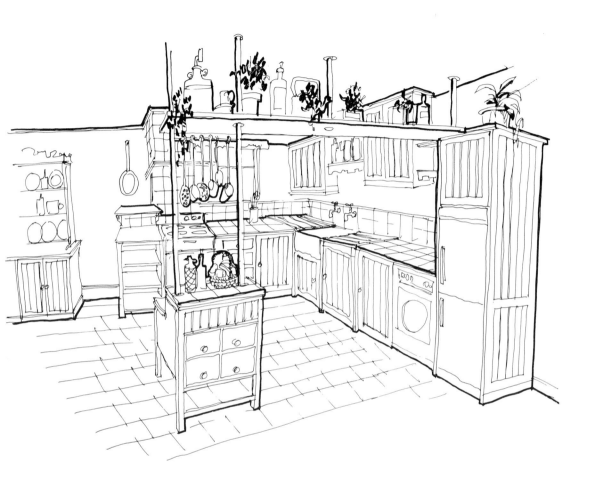

▲ *Figure 28*
The Unfitted Kitchen where standard units are not used

□□□□
Work Tops and Doors

As well as fitting finishes, you must also decide on the finish for your worktop. There are really only three finishes which can be effectively used - the melamine finish, the tiled top and the marble slab. Most units have melamine tops fixed. Tiles are usually an extra if you want them, and come in a range of colours. Marble is more expensive again but makes a lovely worktop. It is marvellous for making pastry.

The most dominant feature of all these units is the doors. They come in two finishes - melamine and hardwood. The melamine door is simple and can have either a plastic edge or a hardwood edge trim. The colours available are rather limited. The melamine panel can also be fitted into a hardwood frame, giving a little of both worlds. The hardwood doors have various types of panels available, depending very much on the actual manufacturer. Most are framed and panelled and these can be either plain or have wavy styles. Figure 29 (colour plate) shows one of those on the market.

One important feature of your units must be the drawers. Some are quite frankly terrible and fall to pieces in no time, while others are excellent. The drawer interiors should be moulded in one piece. You should avoid the type which is normally used in the DIY-type plastic units. These have plastic drawer sides held at the corners with plastic corner pieces and grooved to take a hardboard base.

❏ ❏ ❏ ❏
New for Old

There can be no doubt about it - installing new kitchen fittings is expensive. So maybe you should be thinking of upgrading your old units instead. If your old fittings are not too bad and just need a face lift, then it is far less expensive to do a cosmetic job on them. Figure 30A (colour plate) shows a sketch of typical old kitchen units. Let's look at ways and means to make them look a little better.

The obvious way is to paint them. This gives you a wonderful colour range to work with and you can get almost anything you want. The best way is to paint all the frames in brilliant white so that they are all tied together. Then pick out the doors in a colour. It is best to stay simple, but this does not mean that you have to stick to just one colour. By painting the lower doors below the worktop in a colour, with the doors to the high level cupboard painted a tint of the same colour, you get an excellent result. A tint, of course, is a paler version of the original colour and can be the original colour with white added. This makes for interest, and yet there is a unity about your scheme and all the frames are identical anyway. The sketch in Figure 30B (colour plate) shows what I mean.

If your doors are in poor condition, any amount of painting won't make them look well and you will obviously need something else. One simple way of upgrading doors that are just old is to form panels on the face of them from a timber moulding, mitred at the corners just like a picture frame. Figure 31 gives you an idea of how it will look. It is possible to get these framed panels already cut and mitred. Then all you have to do is to pin and stick them in position. Painting them again can be effective and the panels or even the mouldings can be picked out in a contrast.

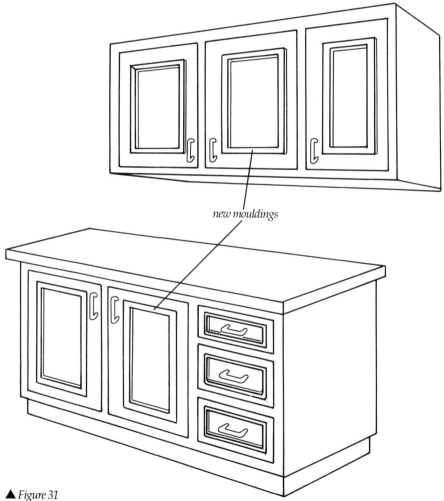

new mouldings

▲ *Figure 31*
Mouldings can be fixed to your existing doors.

If you need new doors, these can be cut from a sheet of chipboard, sheeted both sides in plastic. The edges will have to be covered with something. This can be a strip of plastic which can be obtained and even ironed onto the edges of the doors. Alternatively, hardwood or pine slips can be fitted to all edges. This can look very well, particularly if the door handles are in a similar hardwood. It is possible to get almost any measurement of door you want because they are cut to size.

If you are lucky with your sizes, it may be possible to replace your doors with standard louvered or panelled doors that are generally available at most large hardware shops. It is only possible to adjust the sizes a fraction and your doors must be very close to standard sizes, but the effect can be very gratifying.

It can be quite astonishing what results can be achieved by just the simplest alterations. Even renewing the door handles on all your cupboards can really make a big difference. You should take a look around and see what is available in the shops.

The tops of your units can also be upgraded. The simplest way to do this is by using a preformed kitchen top which has the plastic finish already applied and taken down a curve on the front edge. These come in lengths about 8 feet long in a limited colour range. They are simple to fix and look well and clean. You may find that you have a nasty bit of the end piece showing where a unit suddenly stops and does not go up to a wall. This can be closed off with a plastic strip to give a clean end. A piece of hardwood can even be shaped and fixed to give a slightly better type finish. If you want something special, a small piece of brass can make a beautiful end and is very classy.

❑ ❑ ❑ ❑
Sink Units

If you are renewing the tops of your fittings, perhaps you should consider a new sink unit. There are various types available and all you have to do is to cut a hole in your new unit the correct size and bed the unit down and clamp it in position. Of course you have to contend with all the plumbing as well, but all your services should be there already and will just need connecting up.

Many of these units can now take built-in type preparation boards, drainer units etc. which are simply placed across the bowl so that you can have additional worktop space if needed.

❑❑❑❑
New Walls

A clean-up job can be enhanced by treating the walls themselves. The most popular way is to use tiles. There are many different types, shapes, sizes, colours and patterns on the market and a visit to your local dealer is a must if you are going to consider this. Take a look at several tiles in a group before you make up your mind because sometimes they can look different than just one tile.

Another way to treat your walls is to use timber vee sheeting. This is normally fixed to battens which are fixed to the walls horizontally. The sheeting is just cut to length and pinned in position. This gives a lovely, warm surface. Hooks can be fitted in any position to take many of your utensils or pots and pans. Vee sheeting is the kind of boarding you see on garden sheds. It can be warm and effective when used indoors, especially when used vertically. It can be bought from your local dealer and comes already prepared and just has to be cut to the required lengths.

Redecorating your kitchen is a must when you are trying to get a new effect. One of the problems with kitchens is that the steam and heat tend to discolour paint colours rather badly, white in particular. Where you use white, be sure to use one of the brilliant white ranges so that the discolouration is kept to a minimum. The one surface which discolours worse than any other is the ceiling. I have found that it is better to use a colour on the ceiling so that the discolouration shows up less. Yellows or peach already have yellow in them and so the yellowing process is not noticed so much. The walls are generally best kept in a soft neutral colour to give space and light. A cool blue will reduce the warm effect of the room a little, but is not essential by any means. A lot will depend on the overall effect you are trying to create. The kitchen is an area you will probably spend quite a lot of time in and you should try to avoid bright contrasts and distractions.

Remember!

- Get your circulation right.
- The shape of your kitchen will help you to decide what layout to use.
- Don't forget special units such as the dishwasher or the microwave.
- Gimmicks can be useful, but they won't help poor circulation.
- Make use of 'dead corners' with special corner units.
- Visit several kitchen specialists to see what is on the market.
- If you have money to spare, the unfitted kitchen can be something quite different.
- Look out for different types of work tops and sinks.
- You can often upgrade the fittings you already have.
- Your white ceiling can turn yellow - why not start with a coloured one?

▲ *Figure 25*
The melamine kitchen with hardwood trim (Arco Kitchens).

▲ *Figure 26*
The light hardwood kitchen (Arco Kitchens).

▲ *Figure 27*
The dark wood kitchen (Arco Kitchens).

▲ *Figure 29*
The melamine door is enhanced by hardwood trim (Arco Kitchens).

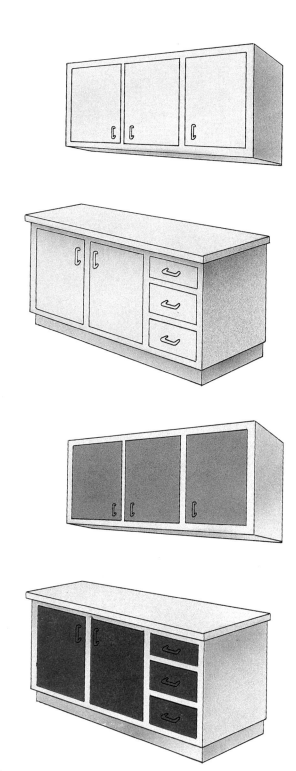

A

B

▲ Figure 30
Doing something with the units you already have.

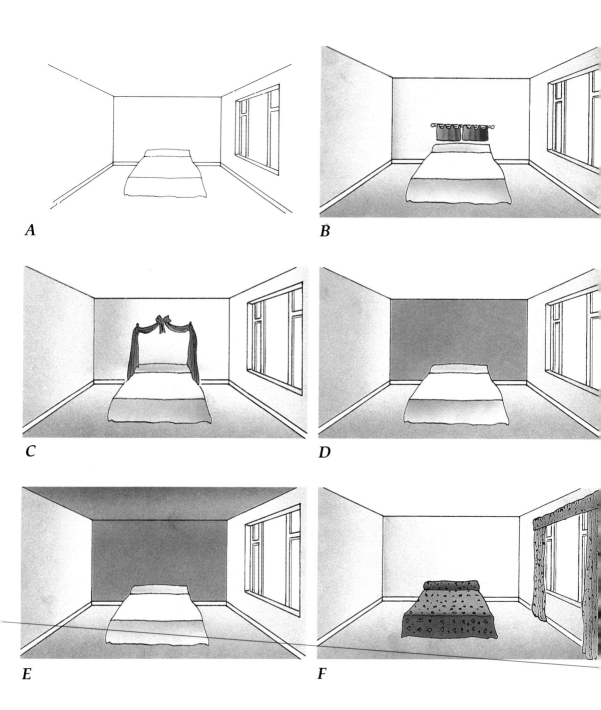

▲ *Figure 32*
Adding impact to the typical bedroom.

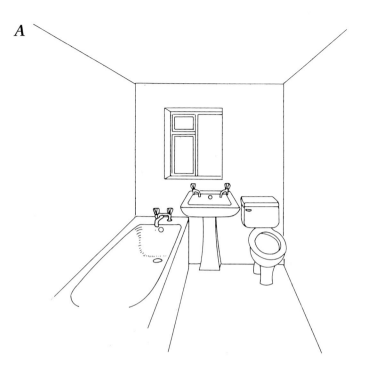

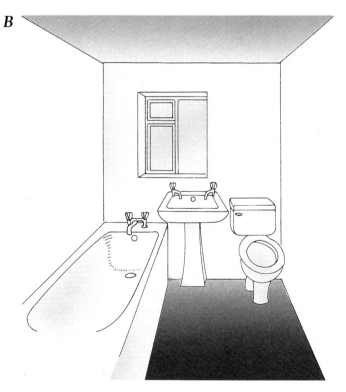

▲ *Figure 33*
Painting the ceiling adds width to the bathroom.

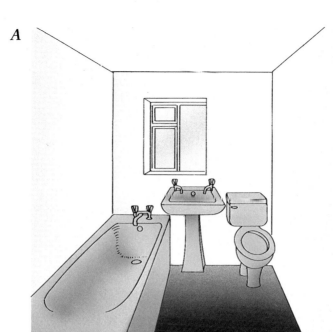

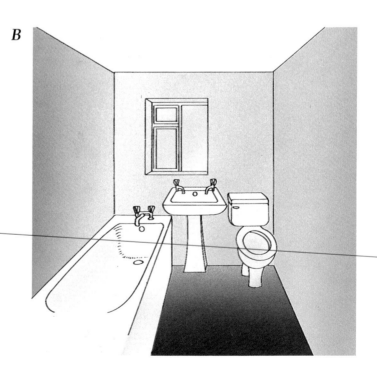

▲ *Figure 34*
The bathroom looks bigger if the walls are darker
than the suite.

9. BEDROOMS

Most modern bedrooms are quite small and the best use should be made of what space is available. The bedroom should be a relaxing room and should not build up tension by having angular patterns and violent colours. The emphasis should be on calmness and by all means on femininity or masculinity, if this is what you want.

The Focal Point

Figure 32A (colour plate) shows an ordinary bedroom in a standard-type house. It has a window wall on one side and has no real features apart from that. Let's take this room as it stands and see what it is possible to do with it to make it look more attractive.

In most bedrooms the bed is the focal point and it should dominate the room. All the features or patterns you introduce should go to make it the most important feature.

What about the bed itself? What can you do to help to make it more important, especially if you have little spare cash? There are varied and many different types of bedhead units available, with or without side tables or lockers. Everything depends on the amount of money you have to spend. Padded bedheads are very popular. They are perhaps the most comfortable of all to use, as there is nothing quite like sitting up in bed reading when you have a bit of comfort behind your back.

Brass bedheads look beautiful and give class to any room, but they do tend to be uncomfortable unless you have oodles of pillows to dull the pain. What if you can't afford an expensive bedhead? A very attractive bedhead can be made by covering pillows with a fabric and forming loops along one edge. A curtain pole can be threaded through the loops and fixed to the wall and there you have a simple, comfortable and excellent looking bedhead. Figure 32B shows how this works.

Simple bedside cupboards can be used, either painted or in natural wood - or indeed any type that suits your purpose. But don't make them work all by themselves. If you use pine ones, for example, try to have a pine dressing table to match, with perhaps a pine curtain pole as well linking everything up and giving overall unity.

With a little imagination, it is possible to use curtains on the wall over the bed to give it more prominence. These can be used in conjunction with a brass ring, such as might be used as a towel ring in the bathroom. Figure 32C gives you an idea of what I have in mind. The results can be both inexpensive and still very dramatic.

Of course a very simple way of giving impact to your bed is to decorate the bedhead wall with a stronger colour or a different paper. This also makes the bed itself look much bigger, as Figure 32D shows. Even greater impact can be achieved by papering the ceiling in a similar paper to that used behind the bedhead, as is shown in Figure 32E. You will notice how the wall and ceiling reinforce each other and give more impact. A pattern on the ceiling is not a bad idea and can be seen at its best from a prone position from the bed. The pattern on the ceiling will also tend to make your room appear larger than it is.

❑❑❑❑
Pattern and Colour

There is a great vogue these days for having curtains and bedspread in the same material, and there are very many different patterns and colours. If you have a large room, these can be effective, but they do tend to cramp a small room and make it appear even smaller. Figure 32F indicates what I mean and shows how both curtain and spread draw together when in the same material. It would make sense if you want to make the bed dominate, and if you want to create space, to make them a little different. There are many co-ordinates available to allow you to do this successfully. If you do this, try to get materials that really have something in common and put the strongest of these on the spread.

One thought you might like to turn over in your mind is this. You look at a curtain from face on - in other words at right angles to it - while the spread is viewed from an oblique angle and would not be as dominant anyway. Bear this in mind when choosing your materials.

If you want to do something smart with your curtains, but don't want them to be too heavy and ponderous, why not use a simple drawn or draped curtain with a matching pelmet? All should be in much the same colour as the wall so that they don't become heavy. Richness of colour and contrast can then be achieved with a strong coloured Austrian blind against the window itself and inside the main curtains. This gives you two curtains in one. Of course it will make it more expensive, but the effect can be staggering.

Another thought is that the bed will practically fill your room and most of the floor will disappear. It would be possible to have a stronger carpet on the floor than you originally thought because much of it has disappeared under the bed. By painting the skirting a similar colour as you did before in other rooms, you gain that little bit more apparent space. A bedroom does lend itself to the use of paler carpet colours, however, and it is possible to get very light shades which will brighten your room up enormously. Indeed entire rooms in very pastel shades can be most expressive and lovely.

❏❏❏❏
Using Mirrors

Space can be gained by using mirrors. It is possible to get mirrored wardrobe doors which slide away and do not hinge into the room. Some people find these pretentious, but they do have their uses. They tend to gain space and they also reduce the visual weight of the wardrobe doors.

If you can help it, don't stand the dressing table in front of the window, since much of the light coming through it will be blocked by the mirror. It is far better to place the dressing table to one side if possible.

When it comes to lighting, I prefer to remove the central light altogether. If you do this, make sure that one light at least goes on when you press the switch by the door. I usually try to have the dressing table light going on in this way. With this and table lamps and bedside lamps, you will have quite sufficient light for normal purposes.

◻◻◻◻
Special Bedrooms

Of course there are many types of bedrooms and each should be treated in its own way.

The nursery is a typical example and this can be a beautiful room. Don't use strong colours on the walls. These may be too dominant for the baby and have been known to make the baby cry relentlessly. Soft off-whites or very pastel tints are suitable. Strength of colour can be added in the way of coloured pictures or borders, or indeed any smaller patches of strength you like. These will not be too violent or strong for the baby. Floor coverings can vary, but many people prefer vinyls or some form of hard materials so that they can be washed down easily if anything is spilt, always a hazard in rooms such as these. If you use a carpet, use a pure nylon one that can be washed or sponged. Lights are better off the ceiling and off the ground and I believe it is hard to beat a few wall lights.

The toddler's room is one that will take a lot of beating and surface finishes should be chosen with caution. The floor covering should be hardwearing, preferably something like vinyl or lino. You will find chewing gum, plasticine and many other matters pounded onto the surface, and carpets just don't like that kind of treatment. Walls should be bright and cheerful. Allow posters and pictures to do most of the work. These can easily be renewed at intervals as the child grows up. There should be boxes or large bins for keeping toys in and these themselves can be in bright colours. Be sure to have some form of table and chair for working and playing at. It is a good idea to have a little anglepoise lamp over the table so that there is good light. Don't forget that this is going to be an untidy room and toys and bits and pieces will be left all over the place. If it is tidy, it is because you probably tidied it yourself. Young children love mobiles that move around in the wind and these can look great in this type of room. Young children love books and comics and it is as well to have somewhere to put these, apart from the floor.

If there is more than one child in the room, bunk beds are space savers. They can be quite magic for young children, although the beds are almost impossible to make. There is no doubt that the new Continental quilts are a must.

Another form of room is the teenager's room. This is quite different again. It may well be that the bed is no longer the important feature here, and the room has become a study room where sleeping takes place as well. A carpet is appreciated. It helps to absorb some of the noise the music will make when the radio or tape recorder is in use. This room becomes a refuge for teenagers, a place away from adults who don't understand them. They will want to express their own tastes and hobbies. Let them stick up posters and record jackets, flags and photos and all the teenage bric-a-brac. Keep the light off the ceiling and give them low anglepoise lamps or table lamps where possible. Book cases are a must and so also is somewhere to study, a decent desk and chair where they can do their homework. They need all the help they can get.

Rooms should express the feelings of the occupiers and say something about them. The bedroom will alter depending on who occupies it, so let the decor help express this.

Remember!

- Allow the bed to dominate the room.
- You don't have to buy a bedhead - it is quite possible to create one yourself.
- Bedspreads and curtains do not have to be the same. Spreads and carpets are seen from an angle.
- Wallpaper and curtains are seen from straight on.
- Two curtains, an outer one and an inner one, can be used for a special effect.
- Mirrored wardrobe doors can increase space and reduce their weight.
- Keep your lighting low.
- Remember what you are doing in the room - make the room suitable for that purpose.

10. BATHROOMS

A Bit More Space

The bathroom is famous for being the smallest room in the house and every conceivable trick should be used to gain a little more space. Although it is the smallest room, you will probably find that it has the same ceiling height as the other rooms. If it is possible to visually lower the ceiling, this will push out the walls and make the room appear bigger. The simplest way to lower the ceiling is to colour it in a strong colour, or even with a patterned wallpaper. Perhaps we better take a look at this in sketch form.

Figure 33A (colour plate) shows an ordinary bathroom with the usual bath, washhand basin and wc. But in Figure 33B you have the same room with the ceiling painted in a colour. You can see for yourself the effect this has, and now you have a wider looking bathroom.

The bathroom can be upgraded in a similar way by putting red deal or hardwood sheeting onto the ceiling. This makes it heavier and drops it in a similar way to the bright colour we just looked at. It does, however, make it look more expensive, although the pine sheeting is not an expensive thing to do. It is also a good insulation material and will help to cut down the effects of condensation.

This illusion can be compounded by colouring the floor in a similar way to the ceiling. This will form a kind of sandwich and will widen out the bathroom even more. Of course you can use the now old trick of painting the skirting colour the same as the floor. In a small space, this is particularly good.

❏❏❏❏
Suites and Tiling

Few people seem to know what the colour of the suite can do for the bathroom - is white as good as a coloured suite? Figure 34A (colour plate) shows a coloured suite with lighter coloured walls. Figure 34B has a white suite with darker coloured walls. This sketch shows quite clearly that the room looks bigger if the walls are darker than the suite. The eye is drawn across the fittings to the wall where the wall is stronger and you get more space.

Walls tiles are most practical in any bathroom and there is an enormous variety available. There are small square ones such as 4" x 4" and 6" x 6" and these are very useful. There are also oblong ones which are about 8" x 6". Most of the colours available are of the pastel type. You can get richer ones, but you usually have to order them specially. There are, however, many patterns to choose from, both modern types and even old Victorian ones which have now come back into fashion. There are even little 2" or 3" border tiles in rich colours and with old mouldings that can be used along with your normal tiles.

Patterns are not only confined to single tiles. There are some which have a pattern spread out over eight or nine tiles to give you a large pattern when all the tiles are up in position. There are also patterned tiles that have plain complementary tiles to go with them. There is no real reason why you shouldn't be able to get what you are looking for.

Let's take another look at our original bathroom in Figure 35A. This time we will concentrate on wall tiles. If you can afford it, take the tiles right up to the ceiling. This is the simplest and cleanest method. Figure 35A shows the tiling to ceiling height. It is sometimes better to take the tiles only as far as the head of the door or the window, about 6'6" high. This will have the effect of stopping the eye at tile height and of course will make your room look larger. Stopping at window height because you can't afford to go any further can be the best solution. Figure 35B shows how the bathroom can be widened out by taking the tiles up to door height only. If you can afford to go right up, why not put in a border tile or patterned tile as shown in Figure 35C. The eye will be stopped at the band and the room will be extended.

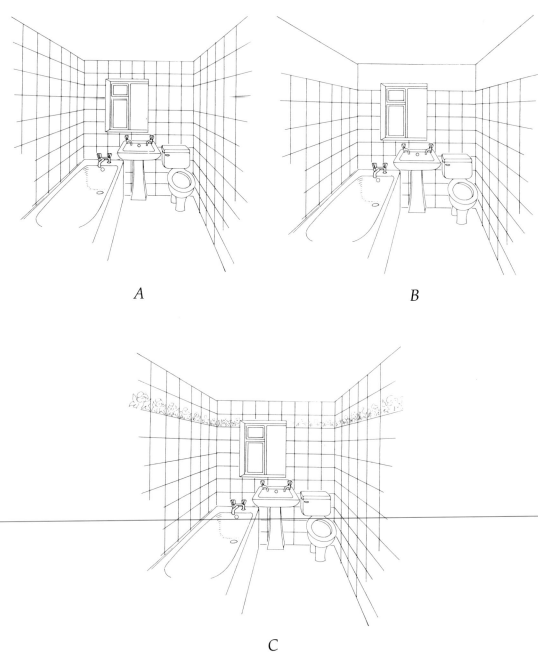

A

B

C

▲ *Figure 35*
Tiling the bathroom and creating space

A tile pattern would need to have a decent space to look anything at all. It is no use cramping it up in a corner somewhere. Figure 36 shows two excellent places for this type of treatment. Go along to your nearest tile suppliers and look around. You will be surprised at what is there to help you. There are even tiles with little bits of a pattern on them such as a straight line or a curved line. By putting these together with plain tiles, you can make up your own patterns and form panels on the wall - almost anything you want.

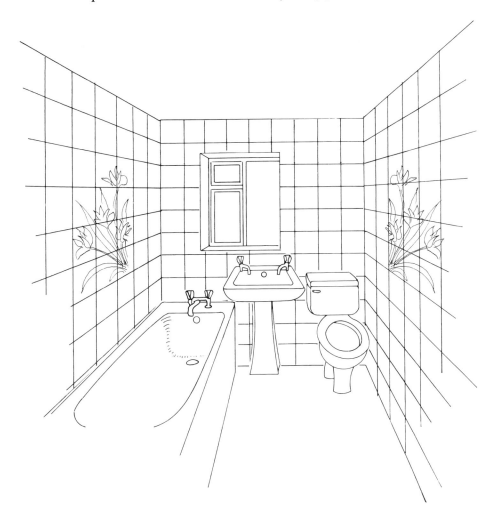

▲ *Figure 36*
The pattern can be made up from a group of tiles like a built-in picture.

◻◻◻◻
Mirrors and Windows

What about mirrors? I like a good sized mirror in the bathroom. The best position is possibly behind the bath. If you make the mirror big enough, you will do wonders for your room. Another unusual place for a mirror is on the side of the bath. This reflects the line of the floor and gives you more space. If you want good light for making up or shaving, a mirror over the washhand basin is the usual position. But sometimes you will find the whb is positioned in front of the window, where it is almost impossible to install a mirror. If this is the case, a small bracket mirror can be fixed to the side of the window return and swung out to use for close work.

Another very annoying thing about some bathrooms is that the window comes across the line of the bath, as shown in Figure 37. You can see how difficult it is to have a bath-shower unit because the window sill catches all the water which subsequently flows out onto the floor. The simple answer to this is to carry your shower rail around the corner and not to stop it against the wall. This brings the curtain back across the window sill and any shower water simply runs down the curtain into the bath.

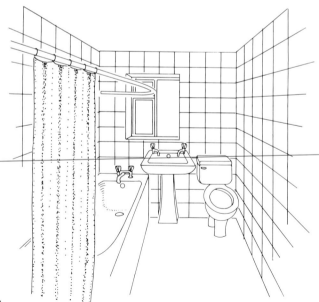

▲ *Figure 37*
The shower curtain rail can be returned across the bath so that water from the shower does not run along the window ledge.

Wet floors seem to be a horror for most people, stopping many a person from putting down a carpet. For the comfort you get, it is well worthwhile - the carpet is only very small anyway. It is possible now to get special carpets designed for your bathroom. They are in nylon on a rubber back and can be lifted and dried or washed when necessary. If you don't want a carpet, try to get a surface which is a little warm underfoot. Cork is very good and has a nice rich colour. It is soft, springy and warm. Lino is also good, but you must lay it in one piece and the floor underneath must be excellent. If your floor is in timber, it is always best to lay waterproof plywood down first to give you a perfectly level surface. Otherwise the lines of your floor boards will show through and eventually wear through as well. There are many types of vinyl and cushion vinyls available and these are also good.

The window always seems to pose a problem for people. They often feel they do not want to hang a curtain because of the steam. I find that a towelling curtain is excellent as it quickly dries out. A roller blind is also very acceptable and nice rich colours can be introduced. The normal thing is to have a net curtain on an expandable spring. This will fill up your window but it won't do much for it. Why not think of an Austrian blind or a cane roller blind?

❏❏❏❏
Other Accessories

When it comes to lighting, most bathrooms have a central light point hanging from the ceiling and that is it. But this gives you very little and does your bathroom an injustice. Is this central point necessary at all? If you can do without it, get rid of it and if necessary put in a downlighter. That will look much better. Try to have a light of some form over the mirror so that you can see what you are doing - but don't have it shining into your face. I have used picture lights with great effect and they look most attractive. You can get a combined strip light and shaving point that can be very useful. If you want to go theatrical, install a batten with small exposed lamps, just like you have seen in the films over the star's dressing room table. These are now on the market and look exciting. If you want to have a light fitting in your bathroom, don't forget that it must have a special pull switch or that it must be switched on and off from outside the door.

To give that special air of luxury, plants are excellent in any bathroom - either at the end of the bath, or even hanging from the ceiling. Many tropical plants such as cheese plants with their slashed leaves thrive in steamy conditions. Your plants can go a very long way to softening the room, giving it personality.

Finally the rich colours of towels do much to dress your bathroom. But if you still feel it lacks something, it is perfectly possible to put a picture or pictures on the walls. There is something a little decadent about this and most people have small pictures or old photos that will look well. A small book shelf or magazine rack is a great extra.

Treat your bathroom like a room and not like the smallest room in the house. Give it personality. Take as long working out the scheme here as you do for any of the other rooms. It really is well worthwhile and it gives you that extra room.

Remember!

- Lowering the ceiling can increase its size.
- Form a sandwich by treating the ceiling and floor in a similar colour and create even more space.
- A bathroom will look larger with pale sanitary fittings against darker walls.
- Visit a tile showroom to see what is available.
- Wall tiles kept down from the ceiling will create space.
- Putting a patterned tile border at top of door height will do a similar trick.
- A good sized mirror can also increase size.
- Make sure your shower water doesn't run along the window sill by returning the shower curtain rail.
- There are special bathroom carpets that don't rot.
- Towelling makes an excellent bathroom curtain.
- Put light fittings only where you need them.
- Some plants like the steamy atmosphere of the bathroom.

11. CREATING MORE SPACE

❑❑❑❑
All done with mirrors!

It doesn't take a great deal of imagination to realise that space can be created by mirrors. It is not always just a simple matter of putting a mirror on the wall and hoping that it is going to give you more room. It doesn't work like that. Mirrors have to be placed with a good deal of care and thought to obtain the best results. Just as with everything else, there are good places for them and bad ones as well.

The two big mistakes people make when using mirrors are in the size used and in the actual reflections received from them. Normally mirrors are made too small and the effects of depth are lost within the outside frame of the mirror. Frequently what is being reflected in a room is not good enough to double up or repeat. Ideally, it is best to be able to reflect the lines of walls, ceiling or floor so that the actual lines appear to be continued into the mirror. It is in this way that additional space can be created most effectively. The mirror must therefore be large enough to go right into the corners, right up to the ceiling or down to the floor — or even into the angle between two walls. Of course any additional space you appear to achieve can be spoilt if you can immediately see your own reflection. This gives the game away and you know right away you are looking into a mirror. This cannot be helped in many instances, but the best results are obtained by carefully placing mirrors on walls at the sides so that it is not immediately evident what is there. The best way of explaining this is by showing you some examples.

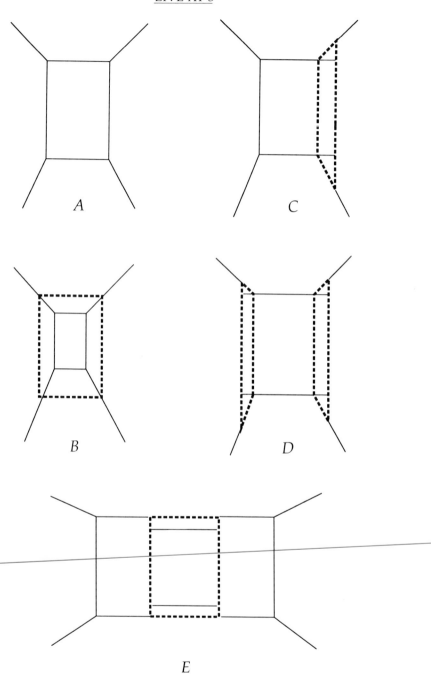

▲ *Figure 38*

Mirrors can be used to create space. In all cases the dotted line shows the position of a mirror. Everything inside the dotted line is a reflection.

Figure 38A illustrates the end of an ordinary room with the end wall and part of two side walls, together with the floor and ceiling. This is rather a narrow room and would be more like a corridor or passage. Suppose we fix a large mirror on the end wall facing us. This is the obvious place to put it, but it also the most unfortunate perhaps. The effect is immediate and the lines of the junction between the side walls and the ceiling and the floor are drawn into the mirror to create depth. The effect is quite dramatic and is shown in Figure 38B. The mirror is shown with dotted lines. Everything within the dotted line is a reflection. It has one obvious drawback and that is that you can immediately see yourself in the reflection - you know straight away that you are looking at a mirror. It gives the game away, but it does double up the length of the room. This can be a disadvantage if you are in a narrow hall, since this treatment would make the hall look much longer and even narrower. One further disadvantage with this type of mirror placement is that it is very easy to walk straight into it and do yourself considerable damage! Many a person has broken a nose in this way. This positioning has uses and if used cautiously, it can be very effective.

Figure 38C is quite clever and can overcome many of the difficulties of the first example. In this example, the mirror is placed on a side wall - once again shown with a dotted line. It is important that the mirror is taken right into the corner, up to the ceiling and down to the floor. The mirror should be no narrower than four feet wide - more if possible. It is a large mirror, but the effects are startling. You will see how the end wall appears to be much wider on one side. It almost looks as if the room goes around the corner and additional space and width are created. The great advantage of this placement is that you cannot see your own reflection and you have no real idea that there is a mirror there at all. It is also not so dangerous because you are not travelling up against the mirror, but along side it. You do not tend to go 'through' the mirror in the same way as in the last example.

It is possible to take this a step further by placing mirrors on the two side walls, one opposite the other. This is shown in Figure 38D, where the dotted lines show the outlines of both separate mirrors with the reflection of each contained by the dotted line. The result is very dramatic. Great width can be achieved at the end of the room or corridor. In fact it appears as if there is almost a doubling up of the space at one end. As in the last example, you cannot see yourself in the reflection, so it is difficult to walk into it. There is an added bonus to this treatment when used in a long corridor. Not only does it widen out the end of the corridor but it also appears to shorten the length of it, so you get additional effects. This is probably the most effective way of using mirrors.

□□□□
Big is Beautiful

There is one important consideration about mirrors, especially when you want to make them large. When you measure up your wall to take the mirror, be careful that the size you choose will actually fit into the house! If you want a mirror on one entire wall, and it works out at 8 feet x 8 feet, you just might not be able to get it through the door. So do be careful. This might sound silly, but it is not half as silly as you will feel when the delivery man arrives. It may be necessary to have a mirror made up from sections rather than in one piece. This would be more economical as well.

Another form of mirror which overcomes the size problem is the flexible mirror called Mirrorflex, which can be rolled up and carried around under your arm. The mirror surface is not in one piece but is made up from many strips or squares or blocks of plastic, all on a flexible back. Mirrorflex is self adhesive with a peel-off back. It also has a transparent peel-off surface to protect the mirror until it is fixed, so do be sure to remove it to get the best results. One advantage of the flexible mirror is that it can be carried around corners. There are various tints available. It can be obtained plain or with light bronze or gold tints. There are even light colours.

Mirrors can also be used in smaller panels but again it is essential to bring them down to the floor, up to the ceiling or against a corner. The reflections should be of lines or surfaces continuing into the mirror. To create space and additional room, you must have lines to reflect. Figure 38E shows how an alcove effect can be created by placing a mirror against part of a wall. Once again the mirror is shown dotted and the reflection is inside the dotted line. See how the floor surface is drawn into the mirror. It is this alone that makes the thing work. If the mirror did not go down to the floor, you would have no reflected illusion.

A strategically-placed object such as a small table or a plant will prevent you from walking into the mirror. You can see yourself in it, of course, but it still looks as if you have an alcove or recess.

❏ ❏ ❏ ❏
Good light reflectors

One further advantage of using mirrors is that they are wonderful light reflectors. If your room is dark, there is no better way of increasing the light available. Daylight can be forced into a dark interior where it would not normally travel.

Some unusual places can be enhanced with mirrors. When used as backgrounds to shelves, they can double up your display.

Inside cupboards can be deepened or brightened. Old-fashioned mantelpieces can have the grates removed and filled with mirrors. This is particularly effective in bedrooms where you would not be normally lighting a fire. Even bedheads can be fitted with mirrors. They can also be used instead of glass in internal doors to give the impression of glass without making it possible to see through. Wardrobe doors are handsome and useful with mirrors fixed. In fact, the uses of mirrors are unlimited!

Remember!

- Mirrors should be large enough.
- Try to reflect lines on surfaces of walls, ceilings or floors.
- Beware of your own reflection.
- Large mirrors at right angles to your line of travel can be dangerous!
- Make sure you can get a new mirror in the door.
- Don't rule out the unusual places.
- Use mirrors to reflect light into your room.

❏❏❏❏
12.BALANCE:
WEIGHT AND SEE

❏❏❏❏
Balancing the Colour

We have already looked at ways of altering the size of rooms by means of colour. Now we will look at how the positioning of colour can alter the entire feeling of a room.

It is quite extraordinary how 'balancing the colours' in a room can affect it. The term 'balancing the colours' seems to suggest that colour has weight and that one colour is heavier than another. Of course, all colours are actually the same weight, but some appear to be heavier than others. For example, a small square of red may look much heavier than a large square of pale blue. Tones can also appear to have weight. A small black square can look heavier than a large grey one. Figure 39 shows this clearly. A strong colour or a deep colour will tend to look heavier than a pale or weak one.

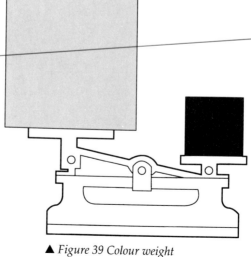

▲ *Figure 39 Colour weight*

In any room it is obviously important to get these balances correct. It is in balance rather than in colour choice that most mistakes are made. If you have a deep rich, red curtain on the window in a room, it must be balanced in some way with something else - otherwise the whole room will appear lop-sided and will be unbalanced. This goes for every kind of room and even every wall in the room.

To show how this works, look at Figure 40A. This shows a typical living room with a chimney breast on one wall and a large window along one wall. It is a simple, normal type of room, the sort that would be in most people's houses. In Figure 40B, you will see the same room but with a heavy curtain across the window. See how the room appears to be heavy on one side. This is most unhappy. If you put a dark, heavy picture or a large piece of furniture on the wall opposite the window, the balance will be restored as shown in Figure 40C. The room will immediately be happier and more pleasant.

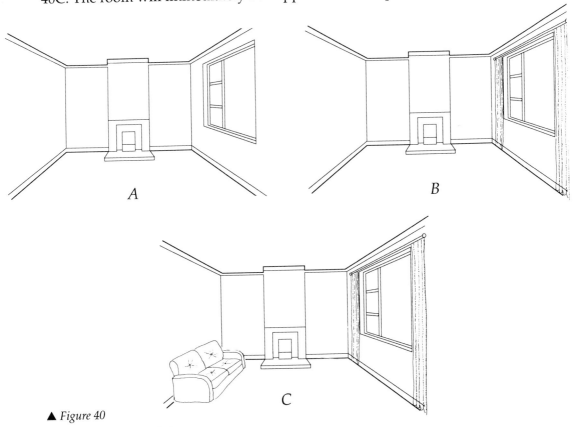

▲ Figure 40

A heavy curtain can unbalance a room.

A wall itself can be unbalanced, so pictures, hangings or furniture should be carefully placed to form a proper grouping. This balance can be achieved in many ways, and a vertical flower vase can balance up a long horizontal shelf. A perfect example of this can be seen over and over again in landscape pictures. In these, a small group of trees at one side of the picture balances the long line of the countryside stretching horizontally across the rest of the picture.

❑❑❑❑
The Centre Line

Balance can be achieved by two means, either by making things the same or by making things similar. Let me look at these in a little more detail.

The surest form of balance is by means of the centre line. This is a very old but still effective method. It consists of creating an imaginary centre line and placing similar objects on each side of it so that complete balance is achieved. This can be most dignified if carried out on a big enough scale. When used in old Georgian mansions it is just perfect. But in the normal modern semi-detached house, it tends to be a little formal and there is not really sufficient room to plan like this. It can still be effective, but it is not easy to achieve a good result without being monotonous or predictable.

In a modern semi, it is usually better to rely on *similarity* of shape or weight to obtain balance. Several small pictures grouped together can balance up one large picture. On a wall, a door at one end might balance up a row of pictures towards the other end. There are so many ways of obtaining balance that the most important factor is to be aware of it in the first place. It is important to balance each wall and then to balance wall with wall until you have a completely balanced room.

❑❑❑❑
Dominant Surface Colour

The placing of dominant surface colours or shades can do a great deal to alter the character and shape of a room. The colours do not have to be in strong contrast to the rest of the room to obtain the best results, but can simply be tonal variations. On the whole, it is when you are not sure of the actual change of a colour that the most effective results can be achieved. Subtlety can be the key to success.

By taking an ordinary room illustration, it is possible to show how simple effects can be carried out to give maximum results.

Figure 41A shows a typical living room, with a chimney breast in the centre of one wall and a window wall on the right hand side. In the following examples, variation is made possible by the use of a single colour tone used in different positions.

Figure 41B shows the same room. But this time an attempt has been made to make the fireplace dominate the room by colouring it on its own in a deep colour. This does two things - it makes the breast narrow and tall, and it splits the room down the centre into two. The narrowness is caused because the breast is coloured in front of a lighter background; the side recesses are lighter than the breast. This, of course, makes the breast appear smaller or narrower, and because of the shape, it makes it appear taller. All in all, the result is a little unfortunate and the breast now sticks out like a sore thumb.

The best way to make the breast dominate the room is to colour the two side recesses in the deeper colour and keep the breast in the main room colour. This is shown in Figure 41C. The sketch shows immediately how this can make the breast much fuller and larger, as well as brighter. The room is no longer split in the centre. In fact, the eye is caught by the lighter colour and skips across the two recesses. If these were coloured with more subtlety and made a deeper tone of the walls, it would appear to make the recesses further away and thus increase space.

There are many variations on this idea of colouring one area in a strong colour which is deeper than that used elsewhere. The following sketches show how these will affect your room's overall appearance. All are quite simple and easy to achieve.

In Figure 41D, one entire wall is deepened, in this case the window wall. This is interesting because there is not a great deal of wall left when you take the window and the curtains out. The curtains, of course, can sometimes make up the entire colour of the wall. Don't forget to take care with what you put on the other side of the room. Although it may well balance the room, it may also compress it with two heavy and strong elements opposite each other. Figure 41E

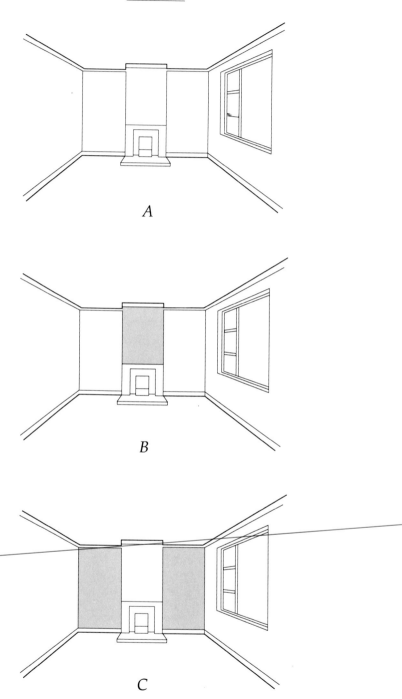

A

B

C

▲ *Figure 41*
Balancing the Room

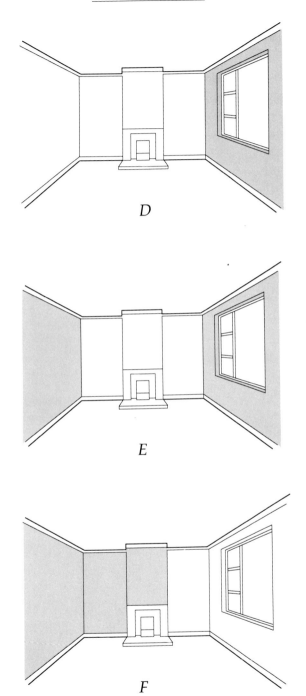

D

E

F

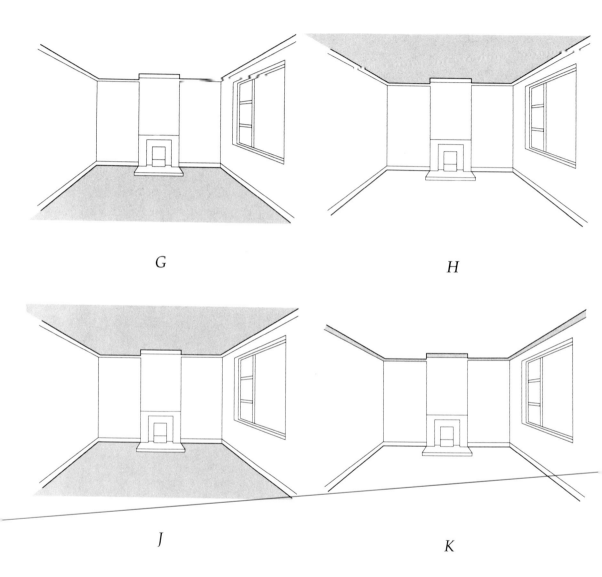

G

H

J

K

shows just how this can happen. When there are two strong colours opposite each other, they tend to draw together and narrow the room. There are times when this treatment can be most successful, particularly when the room is long and narrow and the two short end walls are made to be similar. This works because it is not normally possible to see each wall at the same time - when you are facing one wall, your back is to the other.

Interesting results can be achieved by taking colours around corners. This means that the angle or corner is somewhat lost and not so well defined. This will be easy to see by looking at Figure 41F. Here, the window wall colour is carried on to the recess on one side of the chimney breast. The other wall colour is carried around the room, across the other recess and on to the chimney breast itself. This broadens the room out and its entire shape is changed. If you do this, be careful not to use a dramatic wall colour change. And because they are not related, the room appears to be split up too badly. The two wall colours would be best if they are two shades of the same colour. A relationship will thus be maintained. In this way better balance is achieved. You avoid splitting the room and the results can be most effective and imaginative.

❏❏❏❏
Floors and Ceilings

Weight can often be used effectively on the floor, as in Figure 41G. This can give a good base for everything - walls, furniture etc. - to stand on. If the skirting is painted the same colour as the background of the carpet, an additional few inches can be added to the apparent size of the room because the eye is carried up the face of the skirting. Don't forget that it is better to paint the skirting a colour which is a few shades deeper than the carpet because one is smooth and the other is textured. The smoother surface will look lighter.

This can be effective whether you have a patterned or a plain carpet. Your colour should be similar to the general main background colour. This can help to reduce the general overall height of the room because the skirting and the floor are read together. And while the carpet size is increased, the walls are reduced in height. Care should be taken not to use this illusion where the ceiling is very low.

If your ceiling is reasonably high, placing a colour there can do wonders. Although it can have good impact, once you are in the room you do not in fact look up at all. It will simply act as a coloured canopy, pulling the ceiling down and increasing the rooms size. Figure 41H shows this quite clearly. Unless your ceiling is very high or the room is very bright, don't use too strong or too deep a ceiling colour. The strong colour can draw the ceiling down too much and make it impose itself too dominantly. If the ceiling is a dark colour, it can be extremely depressing to live with for any length of time. Just because you do not look at it, you can still be aware of it and it can affect you psychologically.

The ceiling is normally the best light reflector in most rooms, and colouring can reduce the amount of the light reflecting from it and make the room appear darker. In practice, a soft tint usually works out best. If a room is cold, a warm tint can introduce reflected warmth. A coloured ceiling is particularly good when you have a cove or cornice running around the room at the junction between the ceiling and wall. This should be painted white. In this way, it acts as a perfect foil between the ceiling and wall colours and takes any heaviness out of the scheme. It can also make the room appear smaller because the actual ceiling size has reduced.

Another way to reduce the ceiling height and increase your apparent room size is to fix a picture rail about 15 inches below the level of the ceiling. If the ceiling and wall above the picture rail are all in one colour, the actual main wall colour stops at the picture rail height and space is created. It does take a rather higher ceiling for this to work, and some of the older houses take to this type of solution best.

If space is a real problem, Figure 41J shows a combination of two ideas - to put the same weight colour on the ceiling and on the floor. This forms a kind of sandwich which draws the two surfaces together and expands the room. To work properly, the two areas must be related and have a similar kind of colour. The eye simply reads both of them at the same time. You need plenty of natural light for this, but the results can be quite dramatic. You don't have to use strong colours, only those that are soft and attractive. The deeper the colour, the more the floor and ceiling will draw together and the walls will appear to be pushed out.

❏❏❏❏
Creating Space

If natural light is scarce, and you want to create space, you will need bright or light colours to do it. Figure 41K suggests a simple answer. Here the cornice - the plaster moulding around the top of the walls - is in a deeper colour. This defines the room well and can spread it out. If you don't have a cornice, this effect can be achieved by using one of the many patent paper borders on the market. Some of these can be very effective.

Stencils can also be used with great effect. These have become very popular and there are now stencil kits available in the shops. If you want to go the whole way, plaster or polystyrene coves or cornices can be purchased and stuck up in position. Do be careful, though, because the corners must be mitred at right angles to go around the angles. Your cornice will look terrible if this is not done. It is possible to obtain special corner pieces already mitred so that a very professional-looking effect can be achieved.

You can see just how easy it is to make your room look entirely different just by balancing colours around the main surfaces. The effects can be created by mixing many materials, not just paint. There are an astonishing number of wall coverings and textures available to get any result you may be looking for.

Try looking at various materials that are nearly the same, but not quite. Pick out a textured paper that you like and which you think you can use. Textured paper has a rough surface, rather than a smooth one. Now try to find a paint colour that looks the same. (You will not find it easy because your paper has a lot of depth and shadow due to its roughness.) If you can match the colours up exactly, when you place them on the walls, or side by side, they will look slightly different because one is smooth and the other is rough. To make them appear the same, the paint colour should be somewhat deeper in shade.

It is possible to get co-ordinated papers that are made to go together. One may be a plain paper with a slight texture, while the other may have the same background with a pattern over-printed on it. These are meant to be used together to give variation without contrasting too strongly. Many modern wallpaper books have co-ordinated papers shown side by side. These will give you a good idea of what looks good together. There is no reason why you should stick to the ones shown, however. It is possible to select your own co-ordinates. The suggestions in the wallpaper books are only there to try and help you and give you ideas, and are not meant to dictate to you. After all, you know better than anyone what you like to see together.

Try to pick colours, patterns and textures you personally like. But do try to avoid some of the pitfalls mentioned earlier. Personal taste is important, but it is also important to be sure of what your choice is going to do to your room. Something you like may well make your room appear smaller, and if this is what you want, you have nothing to worry about. If you really want your room to appear larger, think again. Watch out for the ways I suggest you can achieve this and apply your own taste and preferences to that. It can be fun!

Remember!

- Colour has weight.
- Balance each wall by carefully balancing out wall hangings, colours etc.
- Balance each room by balancing out each wall in conjunction with the others and carrying weights around the corners.
- Create variation by mixing textures and patterns.
- Don't rely on taste alone. Think about what your personal taste might do to your room

13. SUMMING IT UP

You know, there's a lot of information in all this. All of the ideas are simple and they do work. It should be possible for you to see just what might happen if you put your personal choice into your home.

Many people become afraid when it comes to doing up their home. Many see something in a magazine or in someone else's house, but they find it almost impossible to recreate a similar effect in their own. They can see a beautiful, strong colour in a photograph and can even find it in the paint shop, but then they tend to get cold feet. They wonder if it will be too strong. They decide to get a pale tint of the colour they liked and the result is that it looks ordinary, not what they wanted at all. That is what I mean by becoming afraid. You do need a little courage. I hope that the ideas shown in this book will help to give you that courage.

Do not throw up your hands in the air and say it is all too difficult. Of course in a little book like this it is only possible to scratch the surface of the subject. You certainly won't know it all even if you master these ideas, but I hope they will help. If this book gives you one or two ideas of how to go about things, then I will be content. I am sure that you may well have come across some of the ideas before. They are not all new but don't let that detract from what they are saying. It is not what you know that counts, but how you use what you know that is really important. This is particularly true of interior design.

This book is not meant to dictate to you. It is only meant to guide you. Take any of the ideas, use them, discard them, vary them and indeed toss them around and use them upside down, but do add your own personal taste and personality to them. This is what this book is really about. It is about *you*. It is about how you live and how you can show that you live. It tries to get you to bring out the fact that you are different from anyone else living down the road. You are unique and your home should say this and express you, not me or my ideas.

A friend of mine had a beautiful house with a splendid living room. It was all most tasteful and well designed but it was perhaps the most uncomfortable room I have ever been in. I felt as if I couldn't relax, or sit back in my chair. Instead, I sat on the edge, ill at ease. The Sunday newspaper was neatly folded and put into the magazine rack. The vase of flowers was beautifully arranged and positioned with exactitude two-thirds of the way along the book case. Everything was perfect - and yet it was terrible. One thing had been forgotten. You have to *live* in the room as well. Don't try for the exotic unless you have an exotic life as well. Try to be yourself.

Don't stop your home at the hall door. Take it outside and show everyone who you are and what you can do. Get any amount of advice you want, but make your own mind up in the long run.

Designing the colours for your own home can be great fun. Don't spoil it by worrying too much. I know that things cost a lot of money these days. Whatever you do, try not to do your room the same as it was before. Don't try to just freshen it up if you can help it. Try to do something quite different.

If you find that it is difficult to finish off your room, for goodness sake don't worry at all. No room should ever be completed. It shouldn't be finished. After all, you are not finished yet, are you? You go on developing new ideas, taking up new hobbies and developing generally. Why should your room stop when you haven't? Keep adding and subtracting and keep it moving. Change your pictures around and shift that chair from the dining room into the bedroom. This will keep it fresh and alive. You really don't have to wait until the spring to go mad and alter things around. Go and meet spring half way and make it early next time.

Finally, you don't have to do up your room on your own. Let the room help you. It has a lot to say if you will only listen. All you need is a little knowledge and some time on your own in the room. Look at it with a new eye and don't be afraid to talk to it. It may well surprise you.

Very best of luck with your decoration. Try things out and experiment. Try to do some of the things you have wanted to do for years but other people have put you off. Go ahead, be a devil and have some fun.